Into the Classroom

Into the Classroom

A Practical Guide for Starting Student Teaching

Rosalyn McKeown

The University of Tennessee Press / Knoxville

Torchbearer Texts
The University of Tennessee Press • Knoxville

Library of Congress Cataloging-in-Publication Data

12.86

McKeown, Rosalyn.
Into the classroom: a practical guide for starting student teaching / Rosalyn McKeown.
      p. cm.
Includes bibliographical references and index.
ISBN-13: 978-1-57233-816-6 (pbk.)
ISBN-10: 1-57233-816-4 (pbk.)
1. Student teaching—United States.
I. Title.

LB2157.U5M37 2011
370.71—dc22
2011011282

Dedicated to Gene, Gary Scott, and Kelsey, from whom I learned so much about teaching, learning, living, and loving.

Contents

FIGURES

TABLES

SIDEBARS

Acknowledgments

This book is the result of many years of interactions with colleagues and students at universities and secondary schools. To them I am grateful. They taught me a great deal about teaching and learning. Sincere thanks go to Bryan Freeman, who was my mentor in my first year of teaching.

Special thanks go to Connie Griffith, longtime friend and editor. Her editing skills are amazing; she smoothes rough sentences and catches details that escape me. Connie's friendship and prayers provide sustenance.

Special thanks also go to the faculty at York University in Canada who piloted the monograph version of this book and to their students who wrote me notes on how to improve it.

Thanks go to Scot Danforth at the University of Tennessee Press, who believed in this writing project and published it.

Author's Note

As a teacher educator, I am aware of the importance that student teachers, interns, and teacher candidates attach to becoming good teachers rapidly. This attention to praxis is admirable, and I want to assist my students in achieving this goal. However, I am also aware that these enthusiastic new teachers need to learn theory and read research-based literature as well as learn about the history and philosophies of teaching, so they can improve over the span of their careers. At times, the immediate needs of the student teachers and the long-term goals of the professors create a tension in departments/schools/colleges/faculties of education. The students focus on praxis and the faculty focus on scholarship. In the end, all of us need to remember that good teaching blends praxis and scholarship.

I wrote this book to help resolve the aforementioned tension. The purpose of this book is to help student teachers, interns, and teacher candidates rapidly advance their teaching skills early in their pre-service teaching experiences. It is my hope and also my experience that this book helps resolve the tension in my methods classes. Because the readers of this text are more skilled and confident in their classrooms, they are willing to listen, read, and learn the theory and scholarship that supports good teaching. The pre-service teachers and I are all winners.

The environment of secondary school is quite different from an office or a university classroom. The pace of the school day is relentlessly fast, with thousands of interactions—student-student, student-teacher, teacher-content, student-content—that the teacher is supposed to observe and analyze with little time to reflect. In the third month of my internship, I wrote in my journal, "I am preoccupied with the daily interactions with the students." This book addresses this common condition; it will help you create a framework for understanding your classroom observations. It will also give you an advance organizer for concepts you will learn in your teacher-preparation classes. By now you (the reader) have taken or are enrolled in initial coursework in human development, educational psychology, and education. This course work is a good foundation; it will help you sort through the jumble of academic and social observations that you make during your practice teaching.

Now that I have told you the purpose of this book, let me tell you what it is not. It is not a comprehensive educational text that reflects the current discourse on major issues facing the education community. This text does not address multiculturalism, students at risk, mainstreaming special education students, social justice, increased testing, or any of the seven "isms" (for example, racism, classism, bodyism). It does not discuss the history of education, the ethical basis of teaching, or the qualities of a good teacher. These topics are addressed in teacher-preparation programs. I hope you will profit greatly from the explanations and discussions of these important topics in your college or university.

We who work in universities are often accused of living in ivory towers and not knowing about the real world. This charge is often leveled at education faculty whose teaching experience was years ago. To get real-world experience of teaching in the new millennium, I recently taught high school for two years. I taught world geography and earth science at one small-town high school of 1,200 students and Spanish in a small rural high school of 470 students. Although I am currently working in a think-tank environment, my high school teaching experience informs and shapes my work. Many of the examples in this book come from my experiences teaching and observing in secondary schools.

Much of this book has been used in monograph form at York University in Toronto since 2000. It has been field tested, and I have received dozens of comments from readers. One comment struck me as worthy of mentioning. Much of classroom praxis is "common sense." I am reminded of a quote attributed to Voltaire: "Common sense is not so common." In our multicultural world, what is common sense to one person may not be common sense to another. If your life experience and cultural background are similar to mine, much of what I write may be familiar to you. However, if your life experience and worldview are different, perhaps you will find this book to be less intuitive and familiar and not based on common sense.

Participating in a school-based assignment (for example, student teaching, internship, or practicum) often comes with uncertainty and anxiety. Common anxieties include: Will I become a good teacher? Will I ever get control of my classroom? My mentor teacher's style is so different from mine; will I get a chance to try teaching my way? How can I do all of this grading and plan for next week at the same time? For those who are in mid–career change programs, student teaching also comes with a lot of reflection on the contrast between your previous career and your new one. During the fourth month of my internship, I wrote a university colleague that I was overwhelmed with observing the thousands of interactions around me—student to student, students with learning, student to teacher—without any time to reflect on the interactions. I also wrote, "I greatly miss the opportunity to think big thoughts and discuss them with colleagues." I wanted to be a good teacher; however, I was so caught up in the busyness of school that I did not have time to reflect and create a larger picture of my teaching and of my teaching within the context of the school, which I felt were essential ingredients for improvement.

Part of the challenge of the initial year of teaching, for me, was bridging the theory and practice of teaching. One of my favorite planning-period activities was to sit with my mentor teacher and talk about things we had observed in my classroom and in the school. We tied together a lot of practice and theory that year. We talked about how students appeared to learn, what they liked, and what they did not like. We related it back to learning styles and other concepts of teaching and learning. We talked about our favorite teachers and why they were good, relating it back to things we had learned from our textbooks. Bridging theory and practice takes reflection. It did not happen when I was in the middle of teaching; it happened only when I had time to reflect, think, and talk.

This book draws on my personal experience and my interpretation of the work of some well-respected authors. I hope that my words and descriptions in some way dovetail with your personal approach to teaching and that they are beneficial to you.

ROSALYN MCKEOWN
NOVEMBER 2010

PART I

Before Entering the Classroom

Chapter 1

Twelve Years as a Student Do Not Prepare You to Be a Teacher

Most adults in American society have spent at least twelve years in school observing their teachers. As a result, they often feel they understand teaching and know how to teach. Good teaching seems effortless to the casual observer and natural to children. Unfortunately, years of observation, especially through a child's or an adolescent's eyes, do not reveal the secrets of the profession. If observation alone created good teachers, excellent teachers would abound in our classrooms. Unfortunately, that is not the case.

Pedagogy is a synonym for teaching. More accurately, pedagogy is the art and science of teaching. Most people think of teaching as neither art nor science. In fact, many people have not considered what makes a good teacher. I have heard it said that excellent teachers are born, not made, and it is true: some people are born teachers. They communicate clearly; organize concepts, facts, and examples so others can understand them; recognize students' needs; create memorable lessons; and exude enthusiasm for learning. These natural teachers have gifts they can develop further to make them excellent educators. I am of the opinion, however, that anyone who desires to can learn to teach. This book is written to help student teachers, interns, and teacher candidates develop basic skills to become better beginning teachers. It is targeted for use during the initial weeks of practice teaching or internship, when student teachers and teacher candidates are anxious to "get off to a good start" and improve praxis rapidly.

Getting started in the classroom can seem daunting. The prospect of teaching while thirty sets of adolescent eyes watch your every move is, frankly, unnerving. This was reemphasized to me at the beginning of a science methods class one afternoon early in Fall semester. After exchanging pleasantries, a prospective teacher asked me what I had planned for the day. While pulling copies of a learning styles inventory out of my briefcase, I answered, "We are going to explore learning modalities and learning styles. You will find out your own learning style and reflect on how it might bias your teaching." The student replied, "I have to teach Thursday! I want to know how to go about it."

In that simple exchange lays the tension. The student wanted to improve praxis immediately. I had planned to work with this cohort of teacher candidates so that at the end of the thirty-week academic year they would feel confident stepping into their own classroom the following autumn. I had not planned to teach to the urgent and real needs of this teacher candidate in her first weeks of school placement. To that end, I wrote this book.

In this text, you will read about different types of learners and how to meet their needs. You will learn how to organize your thoughts into lessons or lectures. You will learn to make your classes memorable, write lesson plans, define objectives, ask questions, give demonstrations, lead discussions, use illustrations effectively, and avoid pitfalls common to novice teachers. All of these skills will help you become a more effective teacher. Consider this book an advance organizer for your teacher-preparation program. The topics covered will be talked about in greater depth in your coursework and your field placement. The chapters in the book can form a skeleton framework so you can hang the barrage of what currently seems like unrelated information from your observations in your school placement, tips from experienced teachers, journal articles, newspaper clippings, ideas from friends and parents, Web blogs, coursework, and the myriad other bits of advice in some semblance of order. The book should also help you understand the scope of the skills you will be required to know and apply in your classroom daily.

I will introduce you to the vocabulary of the education profession. Education, like other disciplines, uses technical terms. By developing a common vocabulary within a discipline, people communicate more precisely with one another. Please note that I am not substituting the definitions of words for presenting teaching skills. For years, I had a sign hanging in my classroom that warns, "Naming ≠ Knowing" (Naming Does Not Equal Knowing). Knowing the vocabulary of a discipline does not guarantee an understanding of the concepts or the ability to implement its skills.

Your teacher-preparation program will include far more than is in this book. It will introduce you to: the ethics and dispositions of the teaching profession; social justice in the classroom; cognitive, social, and physical human development; state and national learning standards; history and philosophies of education; and many digital and print resources for teaching. You might think of your teacher-preparation program as having two halves—classroom praxis and a conceptual/theoretical foundation. Both are important.

Teaching bridges praxis and scholarship. Both are required for professional growth over a career. At this point in your teacher-preparation program, you are probably more worried about the praxis aspect of becoming a teacher. This book addresses your current need. Other textbooks in your program will address your need for scholarship and teach you about the research that underpins good teaching. The purpose of this book is to help you through the initial weeks of your school placement (for example, student teaching, internship, or practice teaching). In this book, I refer frequently to my own teaching experiences in high school and university as well as those of student teachers and interns whom I have supervised. I hope these descriptions stimulate your imagination for things you can do in your classroom and help build your confidence and teaching skills rapidly. As you read, I suggest that you practice the skills presented. Create a mini-lesson in your mind or jot it down on paper. If you are currently teaching a class, try out the techniques. During these experiments, be kind to yourself. You will see improvement over the coming weeks and months. Do not expect to become a great teacher overnight.

Quality Teaching

As I read the teacher certification guidelines for various states in the U.S., it struck me that their underlying purpose is to ensure quality teachers and quality instruction for elementary and secondary students. Quality is a good goal. In fact, quality education is one of the major goals of the global Education for All effort. Also, access to and retention in a quality basic education is the first thrust of the United Nations Decade of Education for Sustainable Development. If you doubt that quality is an educational goal, ask a local school board member if providing a quality education is on her/his radar screen.

Every student teacher I know wants to be a teacher of quality. How you become that teacher and who that teacher is depends a great deal on your personality and your life experiences. It also depends on striving to be an effective professional, now and every year you are in the classroom. Doing so requires staying open to new ideas and ways of teaching. It requires not becoming defensive when your way of teaching something or someone does not work. Yes, I realize that not becoming defensive is a huge challenge. Our pride, professionalism, and approach to teaching are on the line. It is common to become protective of these three; however, we need to realize that our ability to change is an essential ingredient to achieving excellence. I believe that the ability to respond to the rapidly changing world is a hallmark of quality teachers in the new millennium. Classrooms are changing quickly as immigrant populations are growing and technologies alter our patterns of communication and interaction. Being open to and keeping pace with the change is part of being a quality teacher.

Quality teachers are needed now more than ever. In the United States today, the high school dropout rate is about 30 percent. Our Canadian neighbors fare a little better; however, the dropout rate is rising, especially in Manitoba and Saskatchewan. The majority of these adolescent dropouts are destined for underpaid jobs in the service sector of the economy, and for many, a lifetime of low-wage jobs. Keeping children and adolescents in school is much better for the social and economic well-being of our countries.

Becoming a quality teacher is not an easy task. There will be rough spots—times when your preparation for teaching, combined with your coursework, will take all of your time and energy, as well as steal hours of sleep. There will be days in which the ills of society—drugs, abuse, neglect, bigotry, hatred, poverty, violence—spill into your school or classroom. There may be days that you want to quit, but please do not. Quality teachers are, in my opinion, the primary profession that keeps our society viable. The cumulative effects of a teacher's daily contact on the lives of his or her pupils are enormous. Teachers help shape each pupil's worldview, economic potential, and attitude toward others in the community. Teachers educate future leaders, professionals, laborers, parents, and voting citizens. Although teachers are often unsung heroes in our communities, they are our hope for creating a better world.

Getting off to a good start in the classroom is one of the initial steps to becoming a quality teacher. This book is written to help you jump-start your praxis. Happy reading!

REFERENCES

Bridgeland, J. M., J. J. Dilulio, and K. B. Morison. 2006. *The Silent Epidemic: Perspective of High School Dropouts*. The Gates Foundation. http://www.gatesfoundation.org/united-states/Documents/TheSilentEpidemic-ExecSum.pdf (accessed March 1, 2006).

Richards, J. 2009. Dropouts: The achille's heel of Canada's high school system. *C. D. Howe Institute Commentary* 298: 1–23. http://www.cdhowe.org/pdf/commentary_298.pdf (accessed October 19, 2010).

Chapter 2

Common Pitfalls of Inexperience

During your teacher-preparation program, you will hear many descriptions of good teaching techniques; however, rarely will you hear what not to do. This chapter is intended to help you avoid common mistakes as you begin teaching. Following are descriptions and remedies for eleven common errors exhibited by inexperienced teachers: (1) parroting; (2) teaching without first gathering student attention; (3) answering questions for the students; (4) teaching too much in a class period; (5) speaking too softly; (6) claiming classroom success; (7) calling repeatedly on the same students; (8) repeating the same thing in the same way when a student does not understand; (9) introducing informality; (10) tolerating too much disorder; and (11) losing your temper and yelling. I hope these descriptions and remedies will help you avoid these pitfalls. Most of these problems are easy to correct.

In the Author's Note, I wrote that classroom praxis is often viewed as common sense; however, what is common sense to one person may not be common sense to another. The common classroom problems and remedies presented in this chapter may seem like common sense to you. For others, they are revealing. I do not intend to insult your intelligence or your knowledge of praxis by mentioning what may be obvious to you. I simply want to help you strive for quality in your teaching.

Parroting

Just as parrots repeat what they hear, novice teachers tend to repeat student answers for the entire class to hear. This is a bad habit. If you doubt the class heard a student's answer, ask the student to repeat it more loudly. By parroting student answers, you reinforce the idea that only what the teacher says in class is valuable. In effect, you undermine collegial value and trust within your class.

If you have difficulty getting students to speak in a loud voice, increase the distance between you and the student. Students tend to project their voices toward the teacher. When you interact with a soft-spoken student, move backward across the room while maintaining eye contact. You can prompt the student by saying, "Good answer; please repeat that so the class can hear." Usually, the student then feels more confident and will clearly state the answer.

Teaching Without First Gathering Student Attention

Beginning teachers tend to be nervous if their class is talkative or inattentive. Disruptive behavior is especially noticeable and normal in exuberant thirteen- to sixteen-year-olds. I have seen inexperienced teachers trying in vain to talk over the din, steadfastly covering their lesson plans. Afterward, I ask them, "If nobody learned anything, did you teach something?" Then, we have a conversation about gathering the students' attention prior to teaching. It may take one or two minutes, but it is worth the effort because total class learning will increase. See sidebar 2.1 for tips on coping with noise outside your classroom.

SIDEBAR 2.1 Coping with Distracting Noises from Outside Your Classroom

Loud noises outside the classroom are distracting to students and teachers. The noise affects the ability of teachers and students to hear and concentrate. Many elementary schools have rules about conduct in the hallways so that classes are not disturbed. Unfortunately, many other schools do not. How can you teach during unexpected and disturbing noise outside your classroom? If I can control the noise, I stop teaching and tend to the problem. For example, if students are talking outside my class, I stop teaching and close the door to the classroom. If the offenders do not notice me closing the door and lower their voices I add, "Excuse me, I have a class in session, please talk quietly." For noises that I cannot control, I stop teaching until I can be heard and my students can concentrate. For example, if the lawn mower passing outside my classroom window makes so much noise that it drowns out my voice, I stop talking and sit on the edge of my desk waiting for the noise to diminish. I try to see the humor in the situation rather than getting aggravated. I start teaching again when students can hear and concentrate. Continuing to teach when no one can hear you or concentrate makes little sense.

If your class is interrupted frequently by outside noise, talk with your departmental supervisor or principal, who may be unaware of the challenges of teaching in that location and may help you find a solution.

See also chapter 3, "Order in the Classroom," for a description of several methods for gathering student attention.

Answering Questions for the Students

Nervousness distorts your sense of time; five seconds can seem like an eternity if you are standing in front of a class. I have observed inexperienced teachers ask questions, pause for a split second for someone to answer, and then answer the question herself/himself. The students are soon lulled into a passive learning mode, knowing they will have neither opportunity nor obligation to answer.

More-experienced teachers are willing to wait for their students to answer. Students soon get the message that they are expected to respond. If their body language says they are confused, rephrase the question and WAIT. Learning to formulate answers is an important part of the learning process.

Teaching Too Much in a Class Period

Nervousness also makes beginning teachers cover too much material in one class. They may talk too fast, forget to monitor student understanding, or charge through too much material. One student teacher I observed knew he was talking too fast and that the students could not follow. He was in part concerned that he appear to be an expert to the students so they would respect him. He admitted that he ignored the glazed look in some students' eyes and fidgeting in others. In general, teacher talk time is better spent creating a conceptual framework rather than covering a vast amount of facts and figures. If you find yourself lecturing too quickly, slow down by drawing on the board, using illustrations, asking questions, or practicing a relaxation exercise (for example, taking a deep breath).

Speaking Too Softly

Some novice teachers often underestimate the volume necessary to project their voices to the back of a classroom. Because people, jackets, and backpacks absorb sound, speakers must talk louder than normal. Even if you speak sufficiently loud in an empty room, you will need to raise your volume in a full classroom. Often, when I tell my students to speak up, change is barely perceptible. Yet, compared with their conversational voice, they are speaking loudly. The classroom is the place to be theatrical; project your voice to the back of the room.

Claiming Classroom Success

A successful teacher will lead students to discoveries. When students make such discoveries, they own the knowledge and the success. These successes are also a victory for the teacher—albeit a silent one.

One student in my beginning teaching class thought of a clever and memorable way to teach about earthquakes and displacements using green twigs. He led a good interactive discussion and demonstration. At the end, he broke a twig and explained how it was analogous to an earthquake, creating a fault with displacement and aftershocks. As we watched the videotape of his lesson,

---

SIDEBAR 2.2 Social Networking

Social networking is an integral part of society today. Almost everyone I know in the Millennium generation is on Facebook, Myspace, or something similar. Facebook is a great way of sharing photos, news, and fun with your friends. Nevertheless, school districts are taking a careful look at teachers who allow students to have access to their personal Facebook pages. Some school districts prohibit it.

Implications for Facebook and teaching go deeper than the question of giving students access to a personal site. A reality of the job market today is that future employers look at social networking sites. Posting something about your personal life gives others the opportunity to judge your values, behavior, and standards of acceptable conduct. Such scrutiny may have a negative effect on your career. Anything that goes up in electronic format can be made public with far more exposure than expected or wanted when it was posted. For example, if you post and therefore disseminate a conversation with a student or report the conduct of another, you could be violating the Family Education Rights and Privacy Act. Furthermore, such a posting would be unprofessional.

Yes, some teachers create Facebook pages for their students to remind them of reading and homework assignments, post pictures of field trips, and highlight class accomplishments. Such pages can be effective for connecting with students and supporting their homework efforts. Even on these school-based sites, teachers have to monitor what comments students post and must use discretion posting photos (for example, has the parent signed a waiver allowing photos of their child to be taken or published?). Some school districts are creating policies related to social networking sites. Make sure you read the policy before creating one.

---

however, he realized how he had changed the lesson from interactive to teacher centered. Amused and embarrassed, he said, "I was so proud of creating the green-twig demonstration that I wanted to share it with everyone." He continued, "Next time, I'll let the students explain it to me."

By letting students claim the success, you build their confidence as learners. For example, a colleague of mine wistfully shared with me an ironic end-of-the-semester comment from one of her students. The student beamed and said, "I learned a lot in this class." Then, she added almost accusingly, "But you did not teach it to me." Although my colleague, through hard work, had achieved her goal of creating and maintaining a learning environment in which students could be successful, the student felt her new knowledge and confidence as a learner were of her own making.

Calling Repeatedly on the Same Students

Every class has a few dependable students who volunteer answers and who cooperate when called on. It is easy and comfortable to call on these students more than their fair share; however, it is worth the effort to call on more than these few students. You may find you have many talented students in your class if you engage them in discussion.

Some teachers cop out, saying, "I only teach students who want to learn." I always question how these teachers "know" that quiet students do not want to learn. Do they ask: Have I talked to the students about their lack of progress in the class? Have I used a variety of techniques to engage the students through their own learning styles? Good teaching involves accepting the challenge of teaching everyone, not simply those who overtly show their interest in learning. There are many ways to engage reticent students. For example, I knew one girl in middle school who was uncomfortable talking in class but was an excellent note taker. I put her at the chalkboard to record class discussion; she shone in that job.

Repeating the Same Thing in the Same Way When Students Do Not Understand

Inexperienced teachers sometimes use only one way of saying or explaining something. When a student does not understand, the inexperienced teacher may repeat the concept or question louder as if the student had a hearing problem. Repeating once as stated is good; however, repeating it again probably will not clarify anything. Good teaching, in part, relies on the creativity of a teacher to rephrase something so all students can understand. Try to use analogies, examples, and your "mental thesaurus" when rephrasing. Learning to reformulate questions is an important part of the process of learning to teach.

Introducing Informality

Educators who are new to the classroom often are uncomfortable sitting on the teacher's side of the desk. They want to be friends with students, so they dress casually and suggest that students address them by their first name. This usually undermines the students' respect for the teacher and negatively affects the teacher's classroom control. Inexperienced teachers who observe other teachers' dress and demeanor, notice the school culture, and act accordingly do not have as many problems.

There is also a difference between being a friend and being friendly. Being friendly is always in order, but being a friend is not. Most secondary students already have a full peer group of friends and do not need another friend; however, they do need good teachers and role models. Even students who appear not to have friends at school do not need a teacher as a friend; they need a teacher who will talk to them about making friends within their age group.

Tolerating Too Much Disorder

Inexperienced teachers tend to tolerate more disorder in the classroom than do more-experienced teachers. This tolerance may be attributable to their untarnished enthusiasm for teaching, which may result in greater acceptance of noise, inattention, and exuberance. I imagine, however, that it derives more from our cultural custom of not correcting other people's manners in public. Teachers, especially teachers of children and adolescents, have the right to expect—and demand—appropriate behavior in the school setting (Canter and Canter 1976).

Losing Your Temper and Yelling

You have undoubtedly seen someone become angry, turn red in the face, and yell. It is an unattractive sight, and the person often appears ridiculous, out of control, and immature. None of us wants to appear ridiculous, immature, or out of control to our students. Yelling erodes the feeling of safety that students can feel in a classroom and reduces the students' respect for a teacher. I advise you not to yell out of anger.

Of course, students, especially adolescent students, can be vexing. However, that does not give you license to act like an adolescent in response. Instead of yelling, I suggest very stern reprimands that leave no doubt that a student's behavior was inappropriate, that s/he has not met your expectations, and that consequences will follow if you observe undesirable behavior again. Stern reprimands are appropriate—yelling is not.

If you are at the point of losing self-control or composure with your class, invite another teacher to join you to observe. Analyzing classroom behavior is complex, but problem solving with a colleague may provide you with new insight and creative solutions.

Awareness Is 90 Percent of the Battle

The previous descriptions of common pitfalls are meant to help you avoid common mistakes and improve your teaching rapidly. The next time you teach a lesson, check to see if you wander into any of the pitfalls described above. I suggest you observe for and correct one mistake at a time. If you are too busy teaching to self-analyze, record your class on video and view it in the privacy of your home. Once you get past the shock of how you look on video, analyze your style for good and bad habits. After you identify your problem areas, you can then create prescriptions to remedy them. Remember: Awareness is 90 percent of the battle.

Summary

Forewarned is forearmed. In this chapter, I describe eleven common mistakes:

- Parroting;
- Teaching without first gathering student attention;
- Answering questions for the students;
- Teaching too much in a class period;
- Speaking too softly;
- Claiming classroom success;
- Calling repeatedly on the same students;
- Repeating the same thing in the same way when students do not understand;
- Introducing informality;
- Tolerating too much disorder; and
- Losing your temper and yelling.

In most cases, simply being aware of these mistakes will help you avoid them. Good luck!

REFERENCES

Canter, L., and M. Canter. 1976. *Assertive Discipline: A take charge approach for today's educator.* Santa Monica, Calif.: Canter and Associates.

Coaston, J. 2009. Facebook Safety for Students (and Teachers). http://www. stltoday.com/blogzone/the-grade/general-news/2009/08/facebook-safety-for-students-and-teachers/ 8/5/09 (accessed August 10, 2009).

Teachers tread with caution on Facebook. *Tennessean.* August 8, 2009. http://ednews.org/articles/teachers-tread-with-caution-on-facebook.html (accessed August 10, 2009).

ONLINE RESOURCES

About.com: Elementary Education.

http://k6educators.about.com/od/helpfornewteachers/tp/mistakes_new.htm (accessed January 11, 2009).

Yeah, That'll Teach You a Lesson. http://teachyoualesson.blogspot.com/2007/08/ten-rookie-mistakes-of-first-year.html (accessed January 11, 2009).

Chapter 3

Order in the Classroom: Managing Common Discipline Problems

Every new teacher's nightmare is a class that will not listen, talks excessively, moves in and out of their seats at will, talks back, treats their fellow students and faculty rudely, and seems to enjoy it. Unfortunately, discipline becomes a major concern of K-12 teachers in today's schools and of anyone who deals with children and adolescents. Managing a classroom or other teaching environment requires skill. Volumes are written on classroom management from a variety of approaches. This chapter describes some basic classroom management skills.

Most experienced teachers will tell you that the first and most important challenge is gaining and maintaining classroom control. This seems to run contrary to the more theoretical approach of some university faculty, who claim that interesting and engaging instructional strategies will reduce, if not eliminate, classroom management and control issues. My experience is that even the most engaging and interesting lessons will not eliminate the need for classroom management skills. Classroom management problems in today's educational community are a fact of life. You will have to deal with inappropriate classroom behavior; how you deal with it is important. It is better to enter the classroom prepared by planning for classroom management situations before they occur.

Inform Students of Expectations and Rules Early

Rarely do student teachers, interns, or teaching candidates have the opportunity to begin teaching the first day of class in a school year. Usually student teachers take responsibility for classes a few weeks into the term. In this situation, it is wise to use the classroom rules established by the teacher. I suggest, however, that you repeat and reinforce the rules as you take over teaching responsibilities. That way, there will be no doubt about what you expect from the students and what they should expect from you. If you are teaching in a yearlong intern program in a school with block scheduling, you may be fortunate to have responsibility of a class from beginning to end and start teaching on the first school day. Then, you can lay out your own classroom rules, consequences, and procedures. By making your expectations clear at the beginning, you will prevent problems later. See sidebar 3.1 for my classroom expectations.

The consequences, in order, for breaking the rules in my classroom are: a warning, infraction noted in grade book and reflected in behavior grade for the marking period, and disciplinary referral to the vice principal. If undesirable behavior continued after a referral, I called the parents.

My classroom rules and consequences fit my teaching style and the high school where I taught. I realize, however, that my rules may or may not suit you. I admit that my classroom has more structure than the rooms of many of my colleagues; however, it is a place where both my students and I can thrive. Fortunately, students are accustomed to adapting to the various structures created by their teachers as they move from classroom to classroom throughout their day. They know that in some rooms they can socialize while doing their work and in others they cannot. Be sure that your students know the rules, limits, and consequences in your classroom and that you apply them consistently.

Consistency in discipline is important. The students must know what to expect in your classroom from one day to the next. Although I was strict, my students knew they could learn and have fun within the boundaries that I had set. The boundaries of my classroom provided a safe and stable environment for them to learn in. They knew that my discipline and temper were not capricious. For students whose home lives are unstable or marked with anger, abuse, alcoholism, or drugs, a predictable and stable classroom is important.

SIDEBAR 3.1 Dr. McKeown's High School Classroom Expectations, Rules, and General Information

Attendance Expectations

Arrive in class and be in your assigned seat when the bell rings.

Stay in your seat during roll call.

If you are tardy, you need a note to excuse it.

When you are absent, you are responsible for requesting the assignments that you missed.

Classroom Behavior

Respect is important. Respect yourself by not making trouble for yourself. Respect your peers by not interrupting their learning environment.

Respect the teacher by doing what she asks. Respect others by not talking while they have the floor.

Arrive in class with the materials necessary to work: textbook, workbook, paper, and pencil/pen. Sharpen your pencils before class begins.

Stay on task, and do all of your assignments. If you finish your work before others, be quiet. (You may not talk to others who have not completed their assignments.)

No sleeping. (If you want to sleep because you are not feeling well, sign out and go to the nurse.)

Don't talk while announcements are being made.

No horseplay.

No public displays of affection.

Don't mess with other people's stuff. After all, you don't want them messing in yours.

Pick up after yourself and don't leave litter behind.

Leaving the Classroom

Ask permission, sign out, and take a hall pass. When you return to the classroom, write the time on the sign-out sheet.

To go to the restroom, use a restroom pass. Sign out and take your pass with you. When you return, put the pass in the purple box on my desk. (You will receive four restroom passes per marking period.)

Assignments and Grades

Put completed assignments in the inbox designated for this period.

Students are responsible for requesting assignments when they are absent. Note—you are responsible for all work during the time you were absent.

You will receive two late homework passes each marking period. If you turn in a late assignment, staple one of the passes to it.

If you don't make up missing assignments by the interim grade report or by the end of the marking period, the grade for the assignments becomes a zero permanently.

All assignments, quizzes, and tests will be marked number right/number possible. (You calculate the percentage.)

Caveat

Although we live in a democracy, this classroom is a benevolent dictatorship with Dr. McKeown in the leadership position.

About February, when both the gray of winter and the school year appear unending, sometimes students get restless and behavior deteriorates in both the classroom and the hallways. At this point, I remind the students of our classroom rules. For the visual learners, I use an overhead as well as talk them through the major points.

- Politeness is mandatory—you may not cut or insult classmates, teachers, staff, or administrators. Use appropriate language.
- When someone is talking, everyone else is listening. When you want to talk, raise your hand.
- Staying on task is your responsibility.
- You may not leave the room without permission.
- Classroom materials are not to be thrown, shot, or used on anyone (for example, no rocket ships made of paper clips; no writing on a member of the class).

This list uses different language than the detailed list I put out at the beginning of the year; however, it sets the same expectations and boundaries.

Five Techniques

Making the rules and enforcing the rules are two distinct issues. The following are a few classroom management techniques that are simple to implement, and you can use them to reinforce the classroom behavior that you expect from your students.

PROXIMITY

Do you remember talking in class to your neighbor until you noticed the teacher walking toward you? Suddenly, you were all business, hunched over your paper, doing your assignment. Your teacher was using proximity to improve your behavior. Generally, the closer people are to an authority figure the more exemplary their behavior. The presence of a teacher is often enough to correct minor behavior problems.

If space allows, I move about the classroom while I teach; therefore, it is easy for me to teach while standing next to offenders. In one instance, a student with a bad attitude was commenting to the student next to him, disrupting the student's concentration. To stop the flow of comments, I lectured from that side of the room. I had to negotiate past chairs and book bags, but the technique was successful. The comments stopped without a confrontation. The offending student knew I did not want him to talk in class, but I did not embarrass him by saying so. I also did not break the flow of class with a reprimand.

USE THE STUDENT'S NAME AS PART OF THE LESSON

One way to correct behavior without breaking the flow of the class is to use a misbehaving student's name in an example or in a word problem. For example, while you are at the board explaining the conjugation of the Spanish "to be" verb *ser,* you see Jack at the side of the room begin to poke at the boy next to him with his pen, trying to make a mark on his arm. The class seems attentive except for Jack and the boy he is tormenting. You can continue the lesson without interruption and give Jack the message to cease and desist. You simply use Jack's name in the next example: "If I want to say Jack is tall, what form of *ser* do I use? *Soy, eres, es, son,* or *somos?*" Jack will know he has been out of line and is being reminded to behave appropriately. Sometimes this technique elicits a laugh from the class. The students know as well as you do that someone is acting up.

THE VOICE

In the science fiction novel *Dune* by Frank Herbert, the Bene Gesserit Ladies learn to develop "the Voice." With it they command the people to do their bidding. Effective teachers also develop a commanding voice. The voice tends to be lower, slower and carries farther than a conversational voice. The voice tends to grab peoples' attention, and they notice you are serious about your requests (for example, take your seat and be quiet). The voice is a skill worth developing, especially for females whose voices tend to be higher and softer.

The first time I experimented with the voice, I found it amazingly effective. My three-year-old was ignoring my repeated requests to get in the car. I lowered my voice and said, "Get in the car." He immediately looked up in distress, dropped his toy, and went directly to the car. Rather chagrined at his distress, I gave him lots of hugs and thanked him for cooperating. Despite my chagrin, I was intrigued by the effectiveness of the voice. I tried it on my class. It worked; in a few seconds, thirty noisy, post-discussion students transformed into a class ready to listen and take notes.

As people grow anxious, their voices tend to rise. The pitch may go up several notes. Speaking in a high voice alerts the class to the fact that you are anxious. Student awareness of your anxiety will not help you gain classroom control. If you are anxious, try to control the vocal expression of your anxiety by lowering the pitch of your voice.

I suggest you experiment to develop a commanding voice of your own. Remember to lower your voice and speak slowly and clearly. Use the voice sparingly; you do not want to desensitize your students to it. By the way, the voice is not the same as yelling.

SEPARATE DISRUPTIVE STUDENTS

If two or more students repeatedly disrupt class, separate them. Sometimes moving a disruptive student one seat away is sufficient. I did this to a chronic talker in a Spanish class. She pouted about her new location and a day later announced, "You moved me here because you don't like me." I leaned down and whispered to her, "I moved you here because you pull yourself and others off task." That ended the chatting and the pouting. If the disruption is of a larger scale, put the worst offender close to you, and place the other offenders next to students who will model good behavior. The rule to follow here is, divide and conquer—divide the students and conquer the problem.

THE PRIVATE CONFERENCE

If subtle forms of classroom management do not work, it is time for a face-to-face talk. Set up a conference in private after class. "Please, see me after class" is a signal to students that their infractions are serious. You can also use the remainder of the class time to figure out what you are going to say.

A typical conference contains the following:

- If possible, start with a positive statement. For example, "Kai, I've enjoyed having you in class this semester. What has happened these last few days to make you argumentative?"
- Describe the behavior that you find unacceptable and specific instances when you have observed the behavior. Sometimes adolescents are confused: what is unacceptable classroom behavior? In today's multicultural society, the norm at home is not necessarily the classroom norm. For example, some families expect their boys to be aggressive, and they promote tussling, punching, and aggressive language. Having two sets of rules may be confusing. You need to be explicit about your class rules and what you find objectionable.
- Listen to the student. Was the situation she or he describes different from what you thought you observed?
- Tell the student you want her/him to stop the behavior.

- Ask the student if s/he has a plan of action.
- Agree on a plan as well as consequences if the plan is not followed.
- Reinforce the student's many good characteristics.

After a private conference, make sure you greet the student positively the next school day. Give the student the impression that this is another day, and the two of you are starting anew.

Parent Conferences

If you cannot gain the cooperation of a student, try talking with his or her parent. I have found that a short telephone conversation with a parent can bring about positive changes. Start the conversation with a compliment about the child and then describe the behavior you would like changed. For example, "I enjoy John's exuberant personality, but he talks constantly in class. He is off-task frequently and is disrupting the learning of other students." Try being upbeat even if you feel bedraggled.

By the way, these are not easy calls to make. Anxiety and dread accompany many new teachers to the telephone. To ease the nervousness, try practicing your opening line before you dial. Also, remember both you and the parent want what is best for the student. Of course, you and the parent may have two different approaches to achieving that goal.

The Bigger Classroom Management Picture

Successful classroom management is more than exercising a few techniques to extinguish undesirable behaviors. Two things will help you gain control of your classroom. The first is developing the skill of withitness. The second is understanding some overarching concepts that underlie classroom management.

DEVELOPING WITHITNESS

Withitness is the quality of knowing what is going on in the classroom; it is akin to the parenting skill of having eyes in the back of your head. Withitness involves developing the skill of "overlapping," which is "attending to two issues simultaneously" (Kounin 1977, 74). For example, an experienced teacher can observe and deal with classroom misbehavior while answering a student's question. Developing the overlapping skill is difficult for some in the beginning, but, with time and attention, new teachers can develop awareness of the entire classroom.

When I started teaching, I was accustomed to giving my full attention to someone who asked for help or who had a question. My tight focus left the remainder of the class unobserved—an opening for mischief. I had to learn to "widen" my zone of attention to include more than the student I was working with. I learned to keep the class in view while I talked to the student, glancing up occasionally to monitor the room. For example, I stood on the side of the student's desk that allowed me to see the majority of the classroom rather than having my back toward the class. I taught myself to look up and scan the classroom with more frequency as well as listen to classroom noise and silences rather than filtering them out as I listened to a specific student.

I have a few colleagues who have amazing withitness skills. They can tell you what every student in the room is doing. They notice if someone is off task or creating minor vandalism (for example, making spit wads to stick on the ceiling, defacing a desktop, or marking in a textbook) or annoying those around her/him. They are talented teachers.

OVERARCHING CONCEPTS FOR CLASSROOM MANAGEMENT

Here are a few overarching concepts to keep in mind while implementing classroom management techniques.

Correct; do not punish or embarrass. Let us examine the purpose of classroom management techniques. The purpose is to maintain a good learning environment in which everyone can learn. The objective of using the techniques is to extinguish disruptive behavior, while retaining willing students who want to come to class and be productive. If a teacher embarrasses or belittles a student, the teacher has not accomplished this objective. Embarrassing or deflating self-worth can cause resentment, and perhaps retaliation, or mental withdrawal from class. It is important to leave the dignity of the student intact while extinguishing the undesirable behaviors.

Start tight and then loosen up. At the beginning of the school year, I recommend enforcing classroom rules consistently. After the students know the rules and I know the students, I can more effectively interpret the written rules to fit the context and the students. With time, I am able to adapt my enforcement of the rules to fit the personalities of the students and their collective personalities as a class. For example, immediately after lunch, students often are rowdy as they tumble into the classroom full of good spirits from eating with friends. I allow for a more exuberant beginning to classes after lunch than I allow for my other classes. I also interpret the rules for individuals so they can thrive in class. For example, I require that students bring their textbooks to class; however, a few students occasionally do not have theirs. The reasons are not forgetfulness, laziness, or maliciousness, so I simply lend them a textbook. I also do not embarrass the student by asking where the text is, because the truthful answer

Sidebar 3.2 Learning to Do School

Some students catch on quickly to school. They learn the routines and the rules, they figure out what is expected of them, and they behave within acceptable limits. There are other students who miss the subtle and obvious clues and need the teacher's help learning to do school. Helping students can take many paths. One of those paths is clearly stating exactly what you expect of the students. For example, "I expect you to bring your textbook with you to class every day." "I remind you there is no talking during the test, even if you have finished and turned in your examination." "Please turn your chair around and face the people in your discussion group."

Sometimes helping a student to do school requires stating what is painfully obvious to everyone else, except the student in question. One adolescent was infamous at his high school. He had been expelled for a year for drugs and was back in school being a major discipline problem for every teacher and the vice principal. One day I sat down next to him and said, "Gus, I appreciate that you are an individual and create your own path in life, but your defiance of authority is getting in your way here." Sometime later he told me, "I've been thinking about what you said. I can see it." Over the coming weeks his behavior improved and incidences were fewer. He was figuring out how to do school and still be himself.

Other times solutions involve helping students develop the habits of mental and self-discipline that are contrary to their family routine. Getting up every morning to arrive at school on time and doing homework in the evening can be a challenge. In a household where unemployment, drugs, or alcohol is common, the teenager may be the only person carrying out a regular routine of getting up early and doing something in the evenings besides watching television or partying. These students need our support, not simply our disapproval, to learn to do school and to continue to do so against the odds.

is likely too hurtful (for example, Mom and Dad were fighting again last night, and Dad stormed out of the house and drove away with my book bag in the car).

Generally, it is easier to loosen up than tighten up. In the first class meetings, handle infractions as they occur. The oh-it-won't-happen-again-so-I'll-ignore-it approach is often a signal to the student that you are not serious about class rules. More infractions will follow.

The ripple effect. Misbehavior in classrooms tends to multiply and spread across the room. Students monitor the teacher's reaction to infractions of classroom rules. If the teacher ignores a behavior, it can become contagious. Then, the teacher is faced with a more difficult task. If you reprimand the second, third, or fifth offender, you will likely get a protest in response: "Others are doing it." By taking care of infractions early with small signals, like using the perpetrator's name as part of the lesson, the task of classroom control will probably not grow to less manageable proportions.

For example, one student launches a paper airplane. If the teacher does not give a desist notice, another and another may fly. If the teacher only stops the second, third, or fourth perpetrator, the student will likely react with indignation at being reprimanded when the action of others went unmentioned: "So-and-so did it first."

Plan in advance what level of infraction you will allow in your classroom, given your teaching style and personality. At the beginning of the year, you may tolerate few infractions of your classroom rules. As you get to know the students and their habits, you may decide to relax a little. In deciding what behaviors to curtail, think about the infraction and how disruptive it is to teaching and learning. An airplane flying during the last minute of class, as students are putting away their books, is not as disruptive to a lesson as one launched in the middle of seatwork. Will you accept one but not the other? Will one get a verbal reprimand and the other a gentle "no" shake of the head, accompanied by a questioning look?

Also, think about a phrase to use to stop a behavior that has rippled across your room. Singling out one student for a desist notice will appear unfair; giving notice to the entire class that such behavior must stop, however, is a fairer action. "This room looks like JFK airport in New York, with too many airplanes taking off and landing. All further launches are prohibited." The attempted humor serves as an amusing and nonpunitive way to extinguish an undesirable behavior.

Motivation. Motivation comes in two forms: intrinsic (from within an individual) and extrinsic (from a source outside the individual). Of course, the teacher's job would be much easier if every student arrived at school intrinsically motivated and eager to learn; however, that is not the case. Teachers learn to use a variety of motivational techniques and use them with classes and individuals within a class. Some teachers find ways to motivate individual students by linking the task at hand with their personal strengths. For example, a teacher could stop by the desk of a student and drop a positive comment: "This assignment requires attention to detail. You are good at that." "Nice illustration. You are good with color." "Thanks for finding that answer. I'm sure the others in your group appreciate it." "I've seen your determination on the basketball court. If you use that determination now, I'm sure you'll find that answer." Some teachers motivate students with rewards at a later date for current attention on task. For example, "On Friday, we will play Jeopardy if everyone completes the homework packet." As you get to know your students, you will learn how to motivate them individually and as a group.

Graceful exits and saving face. All human beings have egos, which their owners protect. Understanding this will be helpful in dealing with students. One of the covert rules of classroom management is to avoid situations that force students to have to "save face" or prove their toughness, especially in front of their peers. Providing room for a graceful exit can prevent escalation to greater problems. By a graceful exit, I mean finding a resolution that does not create a win-lose situation, but allows the parties involved to maintain their dignity. Perhaps the best thing you can do is to model good behavior, such as admitting your own mistakes, followed by an apology. By doing this, teachers demonstrate they can put their egos aside, accept responsibility, and act from a higher consciousness. Your students will learn much from your actions.

Here is an example of a graceful exit that I gave a student my second year of teaching. A troublemaker had been transferred into my classroom to allow another new teacher the opportunity to develop her teaching skills without constant trials provided by this one youth. I promised the guidance counselor that I would not accept out-of-line behavior from him. The student and I locked horns for several weeks. He tested and I responded firmly. Then, he had two good days in a row in which he was amiable and completed his homework. When he came to class on the third day, I said, "Spring really seems to agree with you. Are you enjoying it?" He agreed that he was. I followed up with, "You seem happier. It must be your season." The behavior problems disappeared for the remainder of the year. With a simple exchange, I had given him a reason for being good; the battle of wills was forgotten.

If several of your students are disruptive, take a good look at your teaching. Are you boring? Are you meeting the needs of your students? Let's face it: if you present interesting classes, students tend to be better behaved. One marvelously creative and fun teacher of high school biology told me that if the students generally have a good time in your class, they will stick with you through short periods of boring material. Ask yourself: what is the ratio of interesting moments to boring moments in my class?

ASSISTANCE

Classroom management is complicated. This chapter is designed to give you a few skills to use immediately in your classroom. If these skills are not sufficient, ask for assistance from an experienced teacher. (Usually, your cooperating or mentor teacher will help you, but at times their personality and management style may be so different from yours that you may need the assistance of another experienced teacher.) Sometimes impartial observers can share their insights with you. The two of you can then approach the discipline problem together. In the course work that accompanies your student teaching or practicum, you will attend classes and read books on motivation, instructional strategies, learning styles, and classroom management. The combination of good instruction, understanding what motivates individual students, and classroom management techniques will more likely keep your class in a learning mode. Discipline alone is not enough.

Time to Grow

Developing classroom management skills takes time and effort; do not get disheartened if you do not develop them immediately. Give yourself time to develop these skills, and work persistently until you develop them. In addition, develop your own discipline techniques—those that work for you and fit with your personality and your way of interacting with others. See sidebar 3.3 for the author's classroom management experience.

Generally, schools have student codes of conduct and handbooks that lay out student rights and responsibilities, discipline policies, and dress codes. These publications inform students and parents what is and is not acceptable behavior. They also describe the layers of faculty, staff, and administration that deal with discipline problems. I encourage you to find out about these policies early in your tenure at a school. By becoming familiar with the conduct code,

SIDEBAR 3.3 The Author's Personal Experience with Classroom Management

Establishing an environment conducive to learning is of primary importance to teaching and learning. Congelosi (1988) describes creating an organized and "businesslike classroom" in which "students and the teacher conduct themselves as if achieving specified learning goals takes priority over all other concerns" (p. 53). How you do this depends a great deal on your personality and your approach to teaching. While teaching high school geography, earth science, and Spanish, I found that teenagers in my classes were more interested in being social than learning. As a result, they would talk to friends frequently, even during instruction and seatwork time. They also came with personal issues and histories. When I stepped into the classroom, I erroneously assumed that everyone in the ninth grade had learned the basics of polite and acceptable classroom behavior. I soon learned that students came with a wide variety of "normal" classroom behavior in part determined by which feeder middle and elementary schools they came from. I found that I had to teach rules of basic respect, and I had to tailor those lessons for individual students. I used parenting skills as much as teaching skills in conveying acceptable behavior to rowdy teenagers.

During the initial weeks of my class, students "learn [ed] to be on task and engaged" (Congelosi 1988, 15). I learned to give explicit instructions during transitions so the class could move more smoothly between activities, with less disruption. For example, when we were preparing to watch a video, I gave the students the opportunity to move their desks. Then, I said, "I expect all of your eyes to be on the screen and for you to be listening, not talking to your neighbor." At first, I was vaguely embarrassed to be stating the obvious expected behavior, but that discomfort soon disappeared when I realized that the students were better behaved when I stated exactly what I expected (Canter and Canter 1976). Also, I gave students a one-minute warning to finish one activity before we moved to the next. This created "transition smoothness," helping them to break their concentration from one task and move to the next (Kounin 1970, 74).

I also cultivated a more personal connection to help students focus on my class. I began every class by asking, "Is there any news I should know"? Students talked about events that interested them about the school, national news, or their friends and family. A few minutes of chat time and public announcements gave everyone an opportunity to talk about things that were on their minds and to connect to me, before we started instruction. Cangelosi (1988) calls this "creating a favorable climate." Jensen (1998, 42) reminds us that emotions are the gatekeepers for learning: "Good teachers who know that emotional climate is critical invest the first few minutes of every class in activities that allow students to get into a positive learning state." Dealing with the emotional climate of the class before beginning instructional activities helps engage students in the classroom and learning.

I also found that laying out the class rules and procedures on the first day of class helped everyone understand my expectations. I displayed the rules, consequences, and classroom procedures using overhead transparencies. I reinforced my expectations frequently during the first weeks of school. Eventually, we got to the point where I could use a Glasser's Control Theory technique. I gave disruptive students a choice: "You have a choice to make. You can continue talking and stay with me one minute after the bell rings or you can quit talking and leave with your friends." The student was then in control of her/his own fate (Glasser 1988). It worked well; I rarely kept a student after class. Two other techniques that worked well for me were to send a signal to the offending student without interrupting instruction. At times I could catch a student's eye and shake my head "no." If that was not enough or I could not catch their attention, I moved to their desk and stood by them while teaching. Proximity usually works (Jones 1987).

My experience with classroom control was that I had to establish order through rules based on courtesy and respect and I had to gain experience before I could see the larger classroom management picture. After I established order and kept it by running an organized classroom, I could then see the theories and management techniques operating in my classroom. (I included citations in this section for some of the authors that have influenced my classroom management style.) It became apparent how positive reinforcement worked with many and how sterner admonitions were necessary for a few. Along the way, I developed "withitness" skills (Kounin 1977). I learned to visually scan my classroom frequently and listen for noise and silence, while attending to other tasks.

With time in the classroom, I moved from managing my classroom by instinct or techniques suggested by another teacher or supervisor to observing and analyzing my own classroom and creating my own solutions. That transformation increased my self-confidence as a teacher.

discipline policy, referral system, and due process, you will be able to function as an integral part of the teaching staff, providing consistent interpretation and implementation of schoolwide policies.

Summary

As a teacher, you will have to deal with misbehaving students. Inform your students early of expectations and rules. Here are five basic classroom management techniques:

- Proximity—stand near the offender;
- Use the student's name as part of the lesson;
- Develop and use a commanding voice;
- Separate the offenders; and
- Schedule a private conference.

Using these techniques will promote and maintain a good learning environment. Remember to extinguish unwanted behaviors before they repeat across the classroom, but leave the dignity of students intact. As you develop your classroom management techniques, think about:

- Correcting students, not punishing or embarrassing them;
- Preventing the ripple effect;
- Motivating students both intrinsically and extrinsically; and
- Tailoring the implementation of your classroom management for the personalities of individual students and the collective personality of a class.

Give yourself time to reflect on your techniques for classroom management, instruction, and student motivation with the goal of keeping the students in your classroom in a learning mode.

REFERENCES

Cangelosi, J. S. 1988. *Classroom Management Strategies: Gaining and maintaining students' cooperation.* New York: Longman.

Canter, L., and M. Canter. 1976. *Assertive Discipline: A take charge approach for today's educator.* Santa Monica, Calif.: Canter and Associates.

Glasser, W. 1988. *Control Theory in the Classroom.* New York: Perennial Library.

Jensen, E. 1998. How Julie's brain learns. *Educational Leadership* 56 (3): 41–45.

Jones, F. H. 1987. *Positive Classroom Discipline.* New York: McGraw-Hill.

Kounin, J. S. 1977. *Discipline and Group Management in Classrooms.* New York: Holt, Rinehart and Winston.

ONLINE RESOURCES

About.com: Secondary Education. Classroom Discipline Resources. http://712educators.about.com/od/discipline/Classroom_Discipline_ Resources.htm (accessed January 11, 2009).

Discipline by Design. 11 Techniques for Better Classroom Discipline. http://www. honorlevel.com/x47.xml (accessed January 11, 2009).

PART II

Classroom Instruction

Chapter 4

Ready, Aim, Teach: Writing Objectives and Lesson Plans

Sometimes teaching is like serving a plate of spaghetti. We teachers offer a tangle of concepts, principles, facts, analogies, illustrations, and theories. From this confusing assemblage, we hope that the students sort out and remember the most important parts. But, how can a student, who does not know the topic, judge what part is important? By writing objectives and organizing our thoughts into lesson plans, we can focus our teaching efforts to "serve" less-confusing lessons.

Four questions form the basis of good teaching. The answers to these questions will shape any lesson, class, or course. As you answer these questions, you begin the road to good teaching (see sidebar 4.1).

> **SIDEBAR 4.1 Four Questions—The Basis for Teaching**
> (1) Who is my audience?
> (2) What do I want to teach?
> (3) How should I teach it?
> (4) How do I know if the students learned what I intended to teach?

Who Is My Audience?

In all teaching situations, you must consider your audience. When I receive a telephone call asking me to be a teacher or a guest lecturer, the first question I ask is, "Who is my audience?" Any information I can get about the audience helps me shape my talk. What age level will I be teaching? Do they have any background knowledge on the topic? Why is this topic of interest to the caller and the students? What type of lesson or presentation has been effective or ineffective with the group before? What is their attention span? Do I need to consider adapting my presentation for students with disabilities? Is there any other information that will help me communicate effectively?

What Do I Want to Teach?

Let us look at the second question, "What do I want to teach?" In most cases, the curriculum is mandated by a state or provincial department of education, and the question becomes, "What do I need to teach?" Answer the question briefly. You should be able to define what you would like to teach in a few key words or a sentence. If your answer is lengthy or you are tempted to say "you know" and wave your hands, then chances are you do not have a clear idea of what you want to convey. In this case, you should rethink the core concepts of your lesson. If you, the teacher/expert, cannot describe clearly what you are going to teach, your lesson will probably lack clarity, and your students will be confused. See examples of teaching objectives in table 4.1. The statements in the left column are *teaching objectives*. The teaching objective becomes the core for the remainder of your lesson. The learning objective is explained later in this chapter in the section "How Do I Know if the Students Learned What I Intended to Teach?"

How Should I Teach It?

The third question, "How should I teach it?" refers to the teaching strategy or method you select to teach your objective. You have many possible strategies and methods to choose from, such as reading, lecture, interactive discussion, worksheet, laboratory activity, simulation, film/video, discovery, or field trip.

Unfortunately, many teachers get in a rut; they repeatedly use one or two methods of teaching. At the university level, teachers usually select lecture, lecture, and lecture. If you are in a natural-science course, the pattern is lecture, lecture, and laboratory. In high school, the pattern is often read, discuss, answer questions, read, discuss, and answer questions. In kindergarten, the pattern is varied—listen, do, discover, talk, and rejoices (see sidebar 4.2.)!

As you develop your teaching skills, you will develop a repertoire of teaching methods and strategies. I like to think of this repertoire as a toolbox. When

---

SIDEBAR 4.2 Rejoice

Rejoice!? Since when is rejoice an instructional method? Well, it is not, but I use it to make a point. Education should be wonderful, fun, exciting, and rewarding. As learners, we should celebrate successfully learning something new to us; as teachers, we need to recognize the efforts of our students. And let us not allow the kindergarteners to have all the fun in learning.

TABLE 4.1 Teaching Objectives and Learning Objectives

TEACHING OBJECTIVES *I want to teach:*	LEARNING OBJECTIVES *The learner will be able to:*
The process of photosynthesis.	Write a paragraph describing the process of photosynthesis.
The application of gas laws to cooling of air with increasing altitude.	Draw and label a schematic cooling diagram showing the expansion and cooling of a rising air mass.
Conjugation of the verb "to be."	Recite the conjugation of the verb "to be."
The use of longitude and latitude.	Identify the longitude and latitude of six major cities around the world.
The differences between Dixieland and Chicago styles of jazz.	Distinguish between Dixieland and Chicago jazz by listening to songs from each era.
The major inequities facing African Americans in the United States, which led to the civil rights movement.	Identify three major areas of discrimination in daily and civic life that stimulated the mass action of the civil rights movement.
The consequences of decades of fossil fuel use.	Graph the rising carbon dioxide levels in the atmosphere.

you have to answer the question "How should I teach it?" you can reach into your toolbox and pull out the appropriate method. Some lessons can be taught best by lecture, demonstration, and practice—for example, manual techniques such as making an icing border in a family and consumer science class. The instructor can briefly describe steps to make a border on a cake, demonstrate the steps, and then let the class practice. Other lessons can best be taught through discussion. For example, you can explore the variety of opinions on an environmental issue in your community through discussion. As a teacher, it is your professional responsibility to thoughtfully choose the method for teaching each objective.

After deciding on an objective and method of teaching a lesson, write down your ideas, so they do not escape you when you stand up to teach your lesson. Stage fright hits all teachers at some time in their careers. Even college professors who have been lecturing for more than twenty years occasionally find themselves nervous as they cover certain topics. New teachers tend to get stage fright with greater frequency. (See sidebar 4.3, Coping with Stage Fright.) One of the symptoms of stage fright is that you forget what you planned to say or do. Another symptom is that you may move too quickly through the lesson so that you skip parts, or you do not give your students time to learn what you are trying to teach. The best way to prevent stage fright from ruining a well-prepared lesson is to write it down. You can write out a script for yourself or outline your lecture and activities. A formal way to record what you are going to do is a *lesson plan*.

Although many experienced teachers do not write lesson plans, it is a practice that helps novice teachers improve more quickly. By writing out a lesson

---

SIDEBAR 4.3 Coping with Stage Fright

A little bit of nervousness can help you deliver a good lesson; however, a big case of stage fright can diminish the quality of your teaching. Here are a few tips for reducing your nervousness before or during teaching.

(1) Practice a relaxation technique that works for you. Some people take a few deep breaths; others focus their eyes and thoughts on one thing. I like to roll my shoulders and shake the tension out of my arms. Focusing on something else besides your anxiety usually helps calm your jitters.

(2) Remember that you are the expert. You have invested hours or years in what you are about to share with the students. Remembering this investment should make you feel more confident.

(3) Often, people have trouble beginning a talk. After a few minutes, they relax and the anxiety disappears. If this is the case, write out in detail your opening remarks. When class begins, read your opening paragraph aloud. It may get you past your initial nervousness.

(4) Distract yourself. If you find yourself growing nervous, try to place your attention elsewhere. Focus on the students, observing them entering the room or engaging a few in conversation.

(5) Practice what you are going to say in spare moments. When I first started teaching, I gave my lecture aloud as I drove to work, took a shower, or washed the dishes. I could experiment with different ways of saying the same thing. Verbalizing helped me develop a speaking vocabulary for my silent thoughts; I admit, this can seem peculiar to the other members of your family or household.

---

plan in advance, you think through your possible future actions in greater detail than if you simply write a flow of activities for the day. Simply listing the flow of major activities, such as "read pages 99–104, answer questions, see video, review major points and discuss video" prompts you to think about the lesson in generalities. Writing a lesson plan helps you think about the details and reasoning behind your teaching. A lesson plan can take many forms. See table 4.2 and sidebar 4.4 for two simple ones.

Sidebar 4.4 shows a lesson plan form that I use for primary school to graduate-level classes. I use this lesson plan format so often that it is in the glossary of my computer. The glossary is reserved for things I use repeatedly, such as my return address, a memorandum form, and a letter closure. I use this format because it gives me the information I need for every lesson, but allows me the flexibility to create a lecture or laboratory activity, lead a discussion, or combine several methods of instruction. Let me explain in more detail what my lesson plan includes.

TABLE 4.2 Sample Lesson Plan Template

Title

What I want to teach (Teaching objectives)	How to teach it (Sequence of instruction)
1.	1.
2.	2.
3.	3.
	4.
	5.
How I will start my lesson:	
How I will end my lesson:	

TITLE

A few key words that describe the content and method.

A glance should tell me the topic of the lesson and the main instructional method. For example, Physical Geography of Europe—Lecture; Solubility—Laboratory Activity; Adhesion and Cohesion of Water—Interactive Lecture with Three Student-Centered Desktop Activities; Mapping the GNP of Eastern European Countries—Guided Inquiry; Latin American Posters—Library and Internet Investigation; Endangered Species—Choroplethic Mapping Activity; and Water Quality—Graphing Activity.

TIME

The number of minutes to teach the lesson.

I often reuse my lesson plans. Writing down the time reminds me that the lesson is a thirty-minute lesson or a ninety-minute lesson. When I am in a hurry, I do not want to read through the entire lesson to remember how long it took to teach. I also do not want to guess and be wrong.

MATERIALS

A list of everything I will need to teach the lesson.

Part of being a good teacher is being prepared. That means having all the materials nearby when you need them. I do not like to discover in mid-lesson that I am missing an important prop, or that I have to stop and inflate a globe. Good lesson plans help the lesson flow without pausing to find supplies. Instruction time and student attention are precious. A little forethought helps you use them efficiently.

OBJECTIVES

A list of teaching objectives.

SAFETY ISSUES

A list of class safety rules and safety equipment to be used in the lesson and a list of steps in the activity that are potentially hazardous. This is especially important for science and vocational-technology teachers.

Safeguarding students is one of a teacher's most important responsibilities. A few well-chosen words can prevent accidents. For example, if students are working with water, I remind them to wipe up spills so the floor will not be slippery—slippery floors cause falls. I also remind them to walk in class; walking reduces the chance of falling. In today's litigious society, teachers must pay special attention to safety. One way to prove that you routinely include safety in your classes is to have it written into your lesson plans.

INSTRUCTIONAL SEQUENCE

A list of the class content and activities in order of appearance.

To keep the sequence of the lesson as I planned it, I list everything I am going to do. For example, I:

- outline the major points of my lecture and include the computer file name of the accompanying PowerPoint presentation;
- list the activities the class will engage in;
- list the questions I want to ask the students;
- describe the demonstration; and
- note the illustrations (for example, graphs or photographs including the computer file names or URL for Web-based illustrations).

SUMMARY OR CLOSURE

A list of the major points I want to make at the end of the lesson.

Because the ending of a lesson is more easily remembered, I write down how I want to finish it (for example, teacher-led summary or student recall of major points). I would rather have a strong, organized finish than a weak and disorganized ending that fails to reinforce core ideas.

EVALUATION

The method I will use to assess student learning (such as discussion, tests, assignments, and so forth).

COMMENTS

Post-lesson notes to improve teaching the next time.

I write a few notes by hand at the end of the day. For example, I note that doing the activity took ten minutes longer than planned, or students were bored by the video. That way, when I teach the lesson again I can make adjustments.

This lesson-plan form works well for me. You can find many other forms in teacher guides or introductory education books at your local library, teachers' center, or teacher site on the Internet. You may want to take a lesson-plan format and adapt it to your needs.

If your school has a lesson plan format they want you to use, I highly recommend you follow it. Trying to "buck city hall" at this initial point in your career is imprudent. You need to build goodwill; being cooperative on non-negotiable items is a good approach.

How Do I Know if the Students Learned What I Intended to Teach?

My lesson plan ends with evaluation. Evaluation brings us to the last question: "How do I know if my students learned what I intended to teach?"

To evaluate whether your students learned what you intended to teach, you must define what you want them to learn. The answers to the fourth question are called *learning objectives*. They become the core to the evaluation of your lesson. Learning objectives are also called instructional objectives or behavioral objectives—they describe the desired terminal behavior of the students. Note that the learning objectives focus on what the student can do; they are *student centered*. The teaching objectives focus on what the teacher presents; they are *teacher centered*. (See table 4.1 for examples of learning objectives.)

Learning objectives should be written so results are observable. The verbs in objectives describe actions, such as: identify, describe, explain, analyze, predict, compute, or demonstrate. Learning objectives should be specific enough to focus the student, but not so detailed that they lead to trivialized learning.

If a stranger came into your class and observed your students, s/he could tell if your students learned what you taught them by asking them to perform the learning objectives you wrote for your lesson. This stranger will not be able to assess student learning if you write objectives with "fuzzy" verbs such as to understand, know, grasp, appreciate, or the like. If you write objectives like this, your evaluation will have to be based on mind reading or looking into students' eyes and intuiting if they understand or not. I have never been good at mind reading; neither are my colleagues. We use observable objectives.

In most instances, I state the objectives for a lesson at the beginning. I do this to help direct student learning. For example, I say something like, "Today you will learn how to write teaching and learning objectives," or "By the end of today's lesson, you will be able to write a lesson plan." By telling my students what I expect them to learn, I alert them to the most important concepts, skills, ideas, and facts in the lesson. They can focus on the important parts of my lecture and recognize that my asides and illustrations are enhanced explanations of the major concepts. The students leave class knowing what I thought was important.

Summary

As you prepare to teach a lesson, remember to answer the four questions:

- Who is my audience?
- What do I want to teach?
- How should I teach it?
- How do I know if the students learned what I intended to teach?

The answers will help you form the foundation for a good lesson.

REFERENCES

Trowbridge, L. W., and R. W. Bybee. 1990. *Becoming a Secondary School Science Teacher.* Fifth edition. Columbus, Ohio: Merrill Publishing.

ONLINE RESOURCES

About.com: Secondary Education. How to write Lesson Plans. http://712educators. about.com/od/lessonplans/ht/lessonplans.htm (accessed January 10, 2009).

Kizlik, B. Adprima. Six Common Mistakes in Writing Lesson Plans (and what to do about them). http://www.adprima.com/mistakes.htm (accessed January 11, 2009).

Park University. Faculty Resources Quick Tips. Writing Quality Learning Objectives. http://www.park.edu/cetl/quicktips/writinglearningobj.html (accessed January 10, 2009).

The Educator's Desk Reference. Write a Lesson Plan Guide. http://www.eduref. org/Virtual/Lessons/Guide.shtml (accessed January 10, 2009).

The Higher Education Academy. Writing Learning Objectives Using Bloom's Taxonomy. http://www.ukcle.ac.uk/resources/reflection/table.html (accessed January 10, 2009).

Chapter 5

Great Beginnings and Endings

Teaching is like preaching a sermon. One experienced country preacher was talking to a novice about how to preach a memorable sermon. The elder preacher said it was easy. The younger insisted it was not. The elder explained his method. "First I tells 'em what I'm gonna tell 'em. Then, I tells 'em. Then, I tells 'em what I told 'em." In this chapter and chapter 7, "Lecture, If You Must," I rely heavily on the advice of the elder preacher.

Research shows that people tend to remember the beginning and the end of sequences. The middle of a sequence is the least memorable. We see examples of this in life. Choir directors will tell you that if the first verse and last verse of a performance are strong, the audience will think the performance was good, even if the middle verses were mediocre. Perform a mediocre beginning or ending and people will notice and remember it. As teachers, we know it is important to have a strong beginning to a lesson and a strong ending. (See sidebar 5.1, Questions for Beginning and Ending Class.) Use the first minutes of the class well. At the beginning of class, we are too often caught up in taking attendance, making announcements, or attending to "administrivia" that we do not focus on the beginning of the lesson. At the end, we may find ourselves too rushed by the impending bell, or distracted by cleaning up, to finish the class well.

Connecting with Your Students

Students arrive in your class with many things on their minds; your lesson is not one of them. They may be thinking about their boyfriends or the girls they secretly admire. Your students may be thinking about the fight they saw in the hall, dealing with the "dis" they just received, or coveting the fashionable outfit a friend is wearing. Personally, I do not care to make the content of my lesson compete with these thoughts. As the teacher, I need to focus students' attention on class and give them a sense of belonging (Jensen 1998). There are many ways to do that. When I taught Spanish, I began class by asking the question, *¿Hay noticias que debo saber?* (Is there any news I should know?) This gave the students a chance to talk about things that were important to them. They reminded me about pep rallies and brought up local and current events. The conversation took one to three minutes and it helped me focus their minds on my class. Then, I could begin the lesson.

Beginning the Lesson

How do you have a great beginning? Some people tell a joke to begin class. My joke repertoire is limited; I rarely have one that relates to the topic I am teaching. Consequently, I have to rely on other ways to capture my students' interest.

Demonstrations, models, questions, and problems are great ways to begin class. One of my student teachers was teaching a physical-science class about waves. To begin class, he had two students stretch a Slinky along one side of the room. He then directed one student to move his end up and down to create a transverse wave. Then, he had one student stretch and release a few of the coils to create a longitudinal wave. The class was attentive. He had effectively hooked the class into the lesson.

The purpose of the beginning of the lesson is to focus the students on the content and process of the lesson. Many names exist for the introductory activity of a lesson. Some of the names are: *set, anticipatory set, focus and review, hook,* and *do now.* The name is not important, the activity is.

Here are a few examples of great beginnings for secondary classes.

- Math—three problems that review skills taught during the past week.
- Science—a discrepant event, such as ice floating in water compared with solid paraffin sinking in liquid paraffin.
- Environmental science: YouTube video TERRA-ble Blues—an environmental pollution song.
- Health—monitor your pulse before and after doing ten jumping jacks.
- Family and consumer science—demonstrate three techniques for preventing fraying on a seam allowance.
- Geography—enact a custom from another country, such as how people greet one another.

Your creativity will help you develop memorable beginnings to your lessons.

After the opening activity, I tell the students the learning objective of this lesson. Often, I also state why this lesson is important. For example, in earth science, I say, "Today we are going to learn about tornados. Given that just last year a tornado tore through a valley close to here, you might want to learn about what causes tornados and what to do if one is sighted." Some students are motivated to learn only if they find the lesson personally important. In a few seconds, I can link today's lesson to their lives or future careers. The results in motivation are well worth the expenditure of time.

Endings

Now, let us move to the end of the lesson, which is called closure or summary. Strong endings are important. Students remember endings to sequences. Unfortunately, endings to lessons are often neglected. Suddenly, the class period is almost over; students are shuffling papers and preparing to leave class. The teacher raises her/his voice, giving last-minute reminders to study for a test or return field-trip forms. The end of the lesson is lost.

The purpose of the summary or closure is to reinforce the learning of the lesson. Teachers can lead the summary, reiterating the major and important points, or ask the students to give the summary. I prefer the second, because the teacher can check the students' understanding of the lesson by listening to the students' comments. One of the best ways to bring closure to a lesson was demonstrated to me by an intern. He led an interactive summary to each lesson. In it, he asked the students what they learned that day. As they responded, the

---

SIDEBAR 5.1 Questions for Beginning and Ending Class

Beginning Class

   (1) How am I going to focus the students' attention?

   (2) What is my objective for the lesson?

   (3) How does this learning relate to the previous or future learning and to the students lives?

Ending Class

   (1) What do I want to review or reinforce?

   (2) What method am I going to use to close the lesson?

intern drew a concept map on the board based on their responses. The concept map provided a visual outline of the lecture, forming a summary diagram.

It is natural to feel redundant recapping the major points of the lesson. I sometimes think, "I just said this point four minutes ago, I feel stupid repeating it." Then I remind myself that from the student's perspective, a review at the end is not redundant. Realistically, my lectures are not so stimulating that the students hang on every word. All students' minds wander off the lecture at some point during the class. My review gives students another chance to hear some information they forgot, or to piece together part of the lecture they missed. Summaries to lessons are important, so make time for them.

Closures do not take long. Two minutes is usually sufficient. Lesson closures are easy; a sharp clock-watcher can finish the lesson closure before the dismissal bell rings.

Summary

Students remember the beginning and the ending of a lesson more clearly than the middle portion. Use these windows of opportunity effectively by planning the opening and closing minutes of your lesson carefully.

REFERENCES

Jensen, E. 1998. How Julie's brain learns. *Educational Leadership* 56(3): 41–45.

ONLINE RESOURCES

About.com: Elementary Education. Lesson Plan Step #2—Anticipatory Set. http://k6educators.about.com/od/lessonplanheadquarters/g/anticipatoryset.htm (accessed January 10 2009).

About.com: Elementary Education. Lesson Plan Step #5—Closure. http://k6educators.about.com/od/lessonplanheadquarters/g/closure.htm (accessed January 10, 2009).

Chapter 6

Instructional Strategies and Techniques: Introducing Variety

Later in the book, I will touch on lecture, models, and demonstrations, and on asking questions and leading discussions as well as interactive teaching. Many other instructional techniques exist. This is a good thing because the cycle of lecture, model, discussion, and worksheets gets a little boring—or monumentally so. In my own high school classroom I like to use: PowerPoint presentation and lecture with fill-in-the-blank notes, discussions, WebQuests, library scavenger hunts, reading assignments with questions, videos with short accompanying worksheets or note outlines, map making (for example, choropleth maps and other colorful mapping techniques), cooperative learning, and worksheets that teach skills and provide practice (for example, reading latitude and longitude and making graphs), simulations, and storytelling. This chapter briefly describes eight instructional strategies and techniques. Hands-on activities, games, and literature can enliven your classroom while deepening or reinforcing learning.

According to Joyce, Weil, and Calhoun (2000, 6), "Models of teaching are really models of learning." The authors put forth one of the best arguments that I have read for varying instruction. They go on to say:

> In fact, the most important long-term outcome of instruc-
> tion may be the students' increased capabilities to learn
> more easily and effectively in the future, both because of the
> knowledge and skill they have acquired and because they
> have mastered learning processes (6–7).

Although there are many ways of categorizing teaching/learning models, Joyce, Weil, and Calhoun use these categories: the social (for example, partnering and role playing), information processing (for example, inductive and inquiry), personal (for example, student-centered learning and nondirective teaching), and behavioral systems (mastery learning and simulations). It is easy to get in a rut teaching with a few techniques that work for you, but let me encourage you to experiment with a variety of other strategies as your confidence and teaching abilities grow.

Hands-on Activities

Hands-on activities give students the chance to "do" as they learn: to experience creating knowledge, exploring, and knowing rather than memorizing a body of knowledge or a history of accumulated facts and ideas. Hands-on activities also help students develop skills (for example, hand-eye coordination or observation skills). Hands-on activities are common in math and science classrooms to help students understand new, unfamiliar, or abstract concepts as well as reinforce concepts introduced previously. Hands-on activities are also enjoyable for many students and serve to motivate them and stimulate interest in both the subject being taught and school overall.

For hands-on and discovery learning, the teacher provides an enriched and supportive learning environment in which students can observe or manipulate materials. Through their curiosity, explorations, use of the materials, questioning, and discussions, students investigate and discover the macro-world around them. Discoveries, such as noticing that bulbs burn more dimly when more than one are connected in a series circuit, have been made by thousands of students over the decades, but the discovery is a meaningful and memorable learning experience for each child.

Examples of hands-on activities include:

- Environmental science: building a soda-bottle compost column and observing decomposition of kitchen scraps.
- Math: making obtuse and acute angles with geoboards and potholder loops or rubber bands.
- Geography: mapping where the clothes in your closet come from.
- Foreign languages: making an articulated paper doll and labeling the major body parts to learn a list of vocabulary words.
- Family consumer science: mixing together baking soda and an acidic liquid (for example, vinegar) to see how leavening works to make quick breads (for example, biscuits and muffins) rise.

Hands-on activities are most effective when the concepts are relevant to students' lives. If students can understand the links between the concepts they study in the classroom and the world they live in, they often are more motivated and have better attitudes toward learning. Improved attitude is often linked to increased achievement.

Storytelling

People of all generations like to hear stories—from great grandparents to toddlers. Cultures around the world use stories to pass life lessons to younger generations. Storytelling has been used for generations as entertainment. On long, winter evenings, people told stories to one another just as we tell bedtime stories to children today. Stories help one generation pass on their societal norms, consequences for inappropriate behavior, traditions, and religious beliefs to another generation.

Storytelling is an effective means to pass information to students and to reinforce ideas they learn from their textbooks. Stories make history come alive and add a human element to otherwise dry information. For example, I tell stories of my international travels. I talk about what places looked, smelled, and sounded like. "When I stepped out of the plane in Lahore, Pakistan, and smelled the wood smoke and dust in the dry hot air, I felt like Dorothy in the *Wizard of Oz*. I thought to myself, 'Toto, we are not in Kansas anymore.'" Later in the lecture/story I continue with the description of the air. "The air held a haze of wood smoke from the cooking fires and dust from dirt roads. It was the end of October; it was still the dry season and there were no rains to wash the air clean. As the haze lingered from one day to the next, it occurred to me that thousands of poor people were not using electricity or gas to cook, but used firewood. At the college where I was staying, I saw men laborers riding home on their bicycles with a few branches of firewood tied on their rear fenders. They were taking the free wood home to their wives to use to cook supper and perhaps heat water for breakfast tea. The air also held the aroma of pungent spices like curry and garam masala used in Pakistani cooking." At that point, I pass around a small container with a teaspoon of curry powder in it. I continue talking about what I ate and what the people wore. I show pictures that I took of everyday things like people riding bikes and motor scooters, sitting and drinking tea, women walking to go shopping wearing their *salwar kameez* with *dupatta* (a long scarf draped around their shoulders and opened down the back), which they pulled over their heads when they enter a mosque. By telling my story of visiting Pakistan, I reinforced knowledge from the textbook about climate, energy use, poverty, food, clothing, and religion. Many students remembered my stories more than the facts presented in their textbooks.

Storytelling is especially good for students whose preferred learning modality is auditory (see chapter 14, "Not Everyone Learns the Same Way You Do").

Here are some ideas for telling stories in different disciplines:

- Science: The history of science is replete with great stories of people making discoveries, such as Alexander Graham Bell placing the first telephone call, or Thomas Edison testing many different materials to use as an element in a light bulb.
- Safety: Every science teacher I know has stories of accidents and near accidents that happened when safety procedures were not followed. For example, someone wanted to know if there was electricity flowing through a wire. Rather than checking to make sure the circuit breaker was off, the student lightly touched the wire, expecting to feel nothing or get a light shock. The electricity flowing through his body made the muscles of his hand contract around the wire and he got a huge shock.
- Family and consumer science: I tell stories of family cooking disasters, such as the day our toddler son, who was watching my husband measure out ingredients into a bowl and stirring them together with a wooden spoon, unexpectedly dumped a large spoonful of baking soda into the cookie dough. My husband did not think the additional soda was important other than that the cookies might rise a bit more, so he did not scoop out the extra soda.
  The cookies smelled great while baking, but they tasted so bitter that he threw them in the garbage.
- History: Among others, you may recall the story of East Berliners streaming through the Brandenburg Gates into West Berlin on November 9, 1989 when the travel ban to West Berlin and West Germany was lifted and the Berlin Wall was destroyed after twenty-eight years of dividing the city.
- Environmental science: Recent history is filled with tales of major conservation projects (for example, dams and roads) and introduction of nonnative species (for example, rabbits into Australia and kudzu into the southern United States) that had unintended consequences.

Cooperative Learning

Cooperative learning is an instructional strategy that involves small groups of students who work together to maximize their own learning as well as the learning of the others in the group. Each group member is responsible for learning the material and also for helping others in the group learn the material. Cooperative learning is **not** the same as group work. Cooperative learning experiences provide five elements: (1) positive interdependence, (2) face-to-face promotive interaction, (3) individual accountability/personal responsibility, (4) teaching and learning interpersonal and small group skills, and (5) group processing (Johnson, Johnson, and Holubec 1994). Research shows that cooperative learning is beneficial to all students, including those who would prefer to work individually and academically gifted students (Johnson and Johnson 1992). Cooperative learning takes many forms; some popular forms include jigsaw, round-robin, roundtable, and group brainstorm.

Jigsaw is perhaps the most well-known form of cooperative learning. Here is how it works. Form heterogeneous learning teams of four—based on academic achievement, gender, ethnicity, race, and so forth—and appoint one student to be the leader of each group. Divide the reading lesson for the day into four segments. Assign each student in each group to read and learn one segment, making sure students have direct access only to their own segment of the reading. The students read their segments twice and then form temporary expert groups of students who have the same reading segment. In the expert groups, the students identify and discuss the main points of their reading and rehearse how they will present to their own learning teams. The expert groups dissolve and each learning team reassembles. Each person in the learning team presents the information from her/his reading segment. The others in the group ask questions for clarification. At the end of the presentations, each learning group takes a quiz or answers a worksheet so that everyone is accountable for the information presented.

Kagan (1994) also has some effective cooperative learning structures. In read-pair-share, students form short-term dyads. One student reads a paragraph aloud and the other student paraphrases it. The second student reads the next paragraph and the first student summarizes it. At a professional development workshop for teachers, I participated in a read-pair-share dyad. The assignment of listening and then paraphrasing made me an active, not a passive, learner. I was astounded at the difference in my own comprehension. I was surprised how many questions I could answer about the paragraph after having been the paraphraser. Read-pair-share is a short task that will help students get accustomed to cooperative learning and help stabilize new learning groups.

One of my favorite instructional techniques for pretest review is to put students into learning teams. I group the students by ability so that competition is level in each group. For example, the top three students in the class are grouped together, as are the bottom three. I make a set of twenty multiple-choice questions that incorporate the major themes and facts important to the unit. I give each learning team one envelope containing the numerals 1–20 on brightly colored squares of construction paper, one set of the twenty multiple choice questions, and one answer sheet. The first student draws a number from the envelope, and the second student reads the corresponding question and possible answers. The first student answers, and the third student checks the answer sheet to see if the answer was correct. If the student gives the correct answer, s/he keeps the number of the question s/he got right; if not, the number goes back into the envelope. The materials rotate clockwise, and the next student draws a number. The process of drawing a number, asking a question, answering the question, and checking the answer continue until all the numbers have been removed from the envelope. The students enjoy this type of review, because it has the atmosphere of a game in which everyone has a chance to learn and prepare for the test, and no one walks away a grand winner or grand loser.

Implementing cooperative learning takes time and patience. Students rarely know cooperative learning structures when they enter your classroom. Teachers must convey to students specific social skills (for example, encouraging others) and specific instructions concerning what the teacher expects in terms of interdependence (for example, everyone in the groups learns) as well as content. Although implementing cooperative learning on a large scale takes considerable thought and effort, a few cooperative learning techniques are easy to implement and can make our jobs as teachers easier. For example, when I do hands-on science, the class can become disorganized, with many students out of their seats asking questions. This is a frazzling experience for teachers, especially new teachers. By assigning roles to each person on a laboratory team, I can keep order more easily. I assign one person the role of equipment manager, another data recorder, and the third task reader/interpreter. The equipment manager is the only one allowed out of her/his seat to get materials or ask questions of the teacher. This simple role assignment reduces the number of students out of their seats by two-thirds and helps with classroom management. By rotating the roles among the students in each laboratory team during the semester, each student will have a chance to exercise different skills and strengths.

I imagine that readers who prefer to learn by themselves are wondering why they should bother learning to implement cooperative learning. Here is one of the best reasons I know. The fastest growing sector of the U.S. economy is the information sector—generating, analyzing, and communicating information—where the norm of the workplace is interdependent teamwork. Interaction among coworkers is vital to complex problem solving that no one could accomplish alone, especially in the fast pace of the international business world. Research within business and industry shows that employers look for prospective employees with good interpersonal skills who can work in teams or on complex projects. According to Kagan, "The most frequent reason for individuals to be fired from their first job is not lack of job-related skills, but rather lack of interpersonal skills" (Kagan 1994, 1:1). Given this reality, it behooves teachers and schools to provide cooperative, interdependent experiences so that students can develop and exercise interpersonal skills that are necessary to support the future economic well-being of current students.

Games

Many of us grew up playing board and card games with our families, neighbors, and friends. We also played games that involved movement, like tag and hide and seek. We were fascinated enough by games to watch people play them on television, like *Jeopardy, Wheel of Fortune,* and the *Price is Right.* Such games can be modified to teach and reinforce concepts in the classroom. Some of my colleagues created specialized game cards for Trivial Pursuit. Others have created Jeopardy games to review for tests. An example of a Jeopardy game in PowerPoint presentation format on exotic invasive plant species can be found on the Southern Appalachian Man and the Biosphere Web site at http://www.samab.org/Focus/Invasive/Curriculum/index.html (scroll down to lesson 14 to download in PowerPoint and PDF formats).

Games that move participants around the classroom, gym, or school grounds are often popular with students. Games such as Oh Deer are wonderful ways of teaching competition, carrying capacity, habitat, and population (Project Wild 2000). In this game students take on the role of deer looking for shelter, food, and water. The students run across the lawn or gym competing to be the first to find their designated requirement in the environment. The deer population increases and decreases as the natural environment's ability to provide food, shelter, and water changes. Games that involve movement are great for tactile-kinesthetic learners who learn through bodily movement and being physically involved in learning (see chapter 14).

When using games in your classroom, it is important to write lesson plans with objectives for the activity. Do you want to introduce concepts or review concepts? Your lesson plan should convey information like:

- Is this an indoor or an outdoor game?
- What are the safety issues?

- What are the objectives of the game?
- What is the social grouping? (teams or individuals)
- How are you going to introduce and describe the game as well as set the rules and rewards?
- What are the rules for the game?
- What are the rewards for learning, applying, or recalling information?
- How are you going to record the results for assessment or evaluation? (How do you know what the students learned? Did they learn what you intended to teach?)

Games are fun and help change the pace and routine of the classroom; however, games must be an integral part of your curriculum and a thoughtful use of instructional time.

Simulations

Simulations are a form of participatory and experiential learning. Simulations are instructional scenarios in which the teacher defines the context in which the students interact. The students participate in the scenario and gather meaning from it. Often simulations are simplifications of complex abstract concepts. For example, Hooks and Ladders from *Project WILD Aquatic* is a simulation of the real-world dangers that salmon face while migrating upstream (for example, fishers, predators, and dams). Students pretend they are migrating fish trying to overcome the obstacles between the ocean and their mating grounds. By their open-ended nature, simulations promote the use of higher-order thinking skills as students contemplate various implications of the context set forth by the teacher. Simulations, because they are distillations of real-world situations, carry with them a feeling of reality and thus engage and motivate students of all ages.

After using a simulation in class, it is important to process the simulation to know if the students learned what you planned for them to learn. I ask the following three questions to process the simulation:

(1) What did you learn?

(2) How is this simulation like real life?

(3) How does the simulation differ from real life?

The answers from the students can be surprising. For example, I had my students play the toothpick game, which is described in sidebar 6.1 to teach about sustainability. When I asked, "What did you learn?" the first group

SIDEBAR 6.1 Simulation: Sustainable Fisheries Management Inquiry

Title: Sustainable Fisheries Management Inquiry (The Toothpick Game)

Description: Sustainable management of a resource pool is complex, involving many social and economic variables. In this game toothpicks represent fish in a lake surrounded by a fishing village. The villagers fish for sustenance and economic well-being. They are challenged to make their resource feed everyone in the village for all times.

Grade Levels: 6–12

Time: 30–45 minutes

Materials: Toothpicks (about 120 per group)

Safety: Remind students not to put the toothpicks in their mouths, because they are germy from being handled by other students. Also remind student that toothpicks are sharp, and the rules of sharp objects apply (for example, do not poke your neighbor with a toothpick).

Objective: To teach about sustainable resource management and that community cooperation is essential to sustainability.

Vocabulary: Sustainable Resource Management, replenish

Instructional Sequence:
• Group class into communities of four.
• Teacher explains that each group of four is a fishing village and that the toothpicks represent the fish in the lake. The village has to figure out how many fish they can catch each round so that there are enough fish for the village to eat forever.
• Teacher explains the rules:
   (1) Begin with sixteen toothpicks (fish) in the lake.
   (2) Each person must draw at least one toothpick per round to survive.
   (3) At the end of each round, "Mother Nature" will replenish the resource pool by approximately one-half of the number of fish existing in the lake.
• Students play the game. If a community does not manage the fish stock well and they die of starvation, request that the students start the game over.

- Question for students to answer while playing: What is the maximum number of fish that each person can withdraw and still have the resource pool last forever?
- Discussion questions for after the game:
  (1) What did you learn?
  (2) How is this simulation like real life?
  (3) How does the simulation differ from real life?

Closure: What did you learn about living in a sustainable community from this activity?

Evaluation: Listen to the discussion of the three questions listed previously, as well as the closure question. The answers are revealing of student understanding.

Extension:

  (1) Play again using individually wrapped candies. How does the simulation differ?

  (2) Ask each student to take on the role of a villager while they play, and tell the others in the group the villager's need for fish. For example, one person may be single and takes only one fish, while another person is married with twins and takes two fish. How would these different roles affect resource management?

Adapted from: To Drain or Sustain? *Education for Sustainable Development Toolkit.* Online at http://www.esdtoolkit.org. Project Learning Tree. 1995. Renewable or Not? Part B Demonstrations, Greed vs. Need: 44–45. *Pre K–8 Environmental Education Activity Guide.* Washington, D.C.: American Forest Foundation.

answered, "It's not possible." I paused before writing their answer on the board. Fortunately, the other groups explained to them that it was possible. The answers to these questions provide the teacher a high level of understanding of what the students perceived and learned during the simulation. The discussion also provides the teacher with the opportunity to deal with any misconceptions that arise.

Listening to CD of Textbook

I assign reading to my students several times per week. I admit, this assignment gets a little old, and for students whose reading skills are not up to grade level, it is a huge challenge. One day, I asked the students if they would like to listen to their reading assignment from a CD that came with the teacher's edition of the textbook. They readily agreed. I played the section, which took about seven minutes; the students were attentive. Some listened, others followed along in the book, and some completed their worksheets while listening. Everyone turned in his or her reading assignment that day. Several students mentioned they appreciated the opportunity to listen. For the students who are auditory learners or whose reading skills are not advanced enough for the textbook, listening to the CD allowed them to extract meaning from the text more easily and leveled the playing field with the visual learners and better readers in the class.

Literature

Poems and prose by great writers are a joy to read and listen to, so I bring them into class to share with my students. When my world geography class was studying South Asia, I brought an excerpt describing colonial India from Rudyard Kipling's "Rikki-Tikki-Tavi" and read it. Although I would have loved to have read the whole thing, I selected two five-minute segments, which the students enjoyed. The prose helped them experience India through a famous author's eyes.

WebQuests

Most students today grow up using a computer and the Internet. Furthermore, their future employment will require computer skills. Accordingly, some classroom assignments should include computer use. For example, a WebQuest makes good use of a computer to help students acquire research skills and stimulate higher-order thinking skills. A WebQuest is an inquiry-based lesson in which most or all of the information comes from the Internet. The task should be doable and interesting. It should have real-life application, such as a scaled-down version of something community residents would do as either citizens or workers (for example, plan a family vacation by mapping travel routes, listing historic places to visit, identifying hotels or campgrounds, and finding places to eat). A WebQuest assignment typically includes: an introduction and background information; a specific task; a list of URLs for Web sites with information pertinent to the assignment, which precludes students from surfing the Web aimlessly and visiting undesirable sites; a step-by-step description of the process that the students should follow to accomplish the task; recommendations for organizing the information acquired (for example, guiding questions or diagrams such as timelines and concept maps); and a conclusion (WebQuest.Org 2008).

Inquiry

Inquiry is a method of instruction that draws on the students' curiosity. Inquiry has a variety of names, such as constructivism and discovery. The amount of guidance the student receives from the teacher varies along a continuum from teacher-guided inquiry to student-directed inquiry. Student-directed inquiry has four parts: identifying what the student wants to learn, identifying resources and how best to learn from them, using resources and reporting learning, and assessing progress in learning (Queens College 2008). Inquiry is more about developing skills, habits of mind, and curiosity and less about transferring of information or mastery of content. Inquiry often involves students learning and using information-processing skills (for example, observing, classifying, measuring, questioning, recording data, inferring, predicting, interpreting data, and hypothesizing). Examples of inquiry include: If you plant a seed upside down, will the stem grow down and the roots up? Why wear a seatbelt in a car?

Instructional Planning

The environmental education community has developed a number of activity guides that contain dozens of activities that use the instruction strategies and techniques described in this chapter. Activity guides like *Project WILD*, *Project WILD Aquatic*, *Flying WILD*, Project Learning Tree, and Project WET are wonderful sources of activities that engage students beyond the common lecture–discussion–worksheet format common in many classrooms.

When I first started thinking about school from a teacher's perspective, I still carried with me my early perceptions of school. From a child's and an adolescent's view, the school year seemed to be endless, with limitless time for learning and teaching. Yet, when I first started to plan my curriculum for earth science, I was struck by how little instructional time there really was. Although school was in session from August through May, the school year was 180 days. By the time I subtracted time for assemblies, pep rallies, club days, in-service professional development, parent conferences, snow days, and so forth, I had about 165 forty-seven–minute periods to teach the rather lengthy mandated curriculum. I learned that instructional time is precious in schools today. Even playing games in class must address some part of the mandated curriculum.

As a new teacher, I wanted to use different things to "spice up" my classroom. The business of being a new teacher limited the time that I had for creativity. I had dreamed of creating a listening station for my auditory students, but time did not permit me to find the headsets and create the tapes. However, what I did have time for was talking to other teachers in my school to find out what they had done. They shared the contents of their filing cabinets with me. Teachers in general are very generous, sharing the teaching materials that they create for their classrooms. The Internet has made sharing possible in even wider circles. I did a simple Google search for "Jeopardy game for teaching secondary school." The search resulted in thousands of Web sites, many authored by practicing teachers, that offer games and activities for classroom use. I performed similar searches for the other instructional techniques listed in this chapter and found hundreds of teaching tips, ideas, and lesson plans. The Internet is fertile territory for new teachers seeking to enrich their curriculums with engaging activities.

In chapter 14, "Not Everyone Learns the Same Way You Do," I describe the many ways that students learn. When you read chapter 14, think back to this chapter. You will see how the instructional strategies and techniques described here engage students of different learning styles and modalities.

Summary

To get beyond the lecture-demonstration-discussion-worksheet format, which is common to many classrooms and schools, you can use a variety of instructional strategies and techniques. These strategies and techniques give variety to your classes while meeting your curriculum goals. They include:

- Hands-on activities
- Storytelling
- Cooperative learning
- Games
- Simulations
- Listening to CD
- Literature
- WebQuests
- Inquiry

When you use these techniques, make sure to write lesson plans with all the basic components (for example, objectives). Although activities based on these instructional models may be more fun, they can and should engage students in learning new concepts or reinforcing previous learning. While giving your students a break from drill-and-practice, the activity still must address some part of the mandated curriculum.

REFERENCES

Cooper, J. M., ed. 1990. *Classroom Teaching Skills.* Fourth edition. Lexington, Mass.: D.C. Heath.

Jacobson, S. K., M. D. McDuff, and M. C. Monroe. 2006. *Conservation Education and Outreach Techniques.* New York: Oxford University Press.

Johnson, D. W., and R. T. Johnson. 1992. What to Say to Advocates for the Gifted. *Educational Leadership* 50(2): 44–47.

Johnson, D. W., R. T. Johnson, and E. J. Holubec. 1994. *The New Circles of Learning.* Alexandria, Va.: Association for Supervision and Curriculum Development.

Joyce, B., J. Weil, and E. Calhoun. 2000. *Models of Teaching.* Boston: Allyn and Bacon.

Kagan, S. 1994. *Cooperative Learning.* San Clemente, Calif.: Resources for Teachers.

ONLINE RESOURCES

California Department of Education. Cooperative Learning. http://www.cde.ca.gov/sp/el/er/cooplrng.asp (accessed July 5, 2008).

Jigsaw Classroom. Jigsaw in 10 easy steps. http://www.jigsaw.org/steps.htm (accessed July 6, 2008).

Kagan Cooperative learning terminology. http://www.journeytoexcellence.org/practice/assessment/cooperative/kagan.phtml (accessed July 5, 2008).

Queen's University. Centre for Teaching and Learning. http://www.queensu.ca/ctl/goodpractice/inquiry/index.html (accessed March 7, 2009).

Project Learning Tree. http://www.plt.org/ (accessed February 27, 2009).

Saskatoon Public Schools. Instructional Strategies Online. What are simulations? http://olc.spsd.sk.ca/DE/PD/instr/strats/simul/index.html (accessed July 9, 2008).

Strasser, B. B., and G. T. Dalis. 1978. Inquiry Teaching Strategies. ERIC ED153972.

Thirteen Ed Online. Concept to Classroom: Workshop: Inquiry Based Learning. http://www.thirteen.org/edonline/concept2class/inquiry/ (accessed March 7, 2009).

What is a WebQuest? http://webquest.org/index.php (accessed July 29, 2008).

Chapter 7

Lecture, If You Must

An educational myth floats about that lecture is the most efficient method of teaching. However, research finds that only about one-fourth of the population learns best from lectures. That leaves three-quarters of the population to suffer through lectures that net them insufficient learning. The lecture is traditional within the European-American educational system. Granted, a lecture covers a great amount of material in a short time, requires few materials, and is as portable as the speaker, but none of these advantages make the lecture the one best way to teach.

Most teachers must lecture at least a little; the most effective secondary teachers give ten- or fifteen-minute mini-lectures. They make a few major points, get the class thinking on a particular topic, and then direct them into another type of activity on the same topic. Whether you deliver mini- or maxi-lectures, the same principles of lecturing apply.

Lecturing is not an effective teaching tool for audiences who cannot sit still, listen, and concentrate for a minimum of fifteen minutes. This chapter is written for people who will be addressing high-school–age and older audiences. That rules out most children middle-school age or younger. This chapter explains basic skills for organizing and presenting a good lecture.

Organization

Have you ever attended a lecture in which the professor did so many asides and jumped around from topic to topic so often that you were not sure what the major points of the lecture were? In such a situation, many students blame themselves for not comprehending. They often assume that the teacher is brilliant and that their own inadequacy prevented them from following the lecture. The fault, however, often lies not with the students but with the lecture.

An informative lecture starts with clear objectives, so begin by writing down your teaching objectives. Teaching objectives mirror the major concepts of your lecture. Then, list other supporting concepts of lesser importance that complement the major concepts. Use these two sets of concepts to form the framework of your lesson. To this framework, you will anchor examples, data, illustrations, and descriptions that will explain the topic and create your lecture.

I assume you are an expert in your field and can select important concepts for your lecture. Experts, however, cannot be knowledgeable in all fields. Occasionally, we must lecture on topics with which we have some familiarity but not expertise. In this case, I suggest you consult with experts to gain insight into the most important concepts. Rarely will you know such an expert personally; however, a trip to the library will put such knowledge at your fingertips. Find a textbook on the topic in question, and open it to the table of contents. The headings and subheadings are most likely the major and supporting concepts you need for the framework of your lecture. The concepts are usually sequenced in an order you can use in your lecture. One of my favorite references for teaching geography and science is the *World Book* encyclopedia. The depth of explanation and breadth of coverage is good for high school audiences.

Personally, I like to outline my lectures. The major concepts become the Roman numeral headings. Supporting concepts become the capital letter subheadings. Then, I add facts, interesting data, case studies, and life experiences to round out the lecture.

I have tried to script my lectures, but I am less successful using a script than when I use an outline. In a script, I write out my lines verbatim. A script allows me to choose my words carefully. Generally, scripts are too detailed for my lecture style. When space permits, I like to walk around the room while I am lecturing. This puts me closer to students who choose to distance themselves from the lecturer. I tend to leave my notes on the podium as I lecture. I ask students for their experience or opinions on the topic I am covering. Through my movements and questions, I try to keep students engaged as active learners. I admit that sometimes I forget the planned flow of my lecture and have to return to the podium to refresh my memory, but this break of a few seconds gives the students time to process the information just presented.

When I lecture, I talk about the interrelationships between major points. The interrelationships may be obvious to me, but they may not be obvious to my students, who have less experience on the topic. Also, I relate the material to previous learning and give sneak previews of what is to come in future lectures. By briefly showing how the material I present is tied to past and future learning, I increase the value of my lecture. Transfer of learning from one lecture to another is a difficult thinking process. A good teacher helps students make those connections.

Road Maps

Remember the minister's advice? Tell them what you are going to tell them, tell them, and tell them what you told them. In effect, telling them what you are going to tell them is giving the learner a road map of where you are going in the lecture. I love to guess what is going to happen next when listening to murder mysteries while I commute, but I dislike putting any energy into guessing where the lecturer is going when I am learning new material. One of my students commented that she really liked the lectures of one geography professor on campus. The student said the professor put an outline of her lecture on the board for every class. The outline helped her follow the lecture and also made a good study sheet for the examinations.

Lecturers often mistakenly assume that the structure and flow of their lectures are obvious to students. However, the structure may be obvious to the lecturer but not to the student. You can convey to the students the structure of the lecture through signposts, which are indicators of the direction of the lecture. At the beginning, you can tell the students the number of major concepts you will be teaching. Each time you start a new concept you can introduce it by saying something akin to, "The second major concept is. . . ." This short phrase will distinguish between major concepts, supporting concepts, and illustrations. Signposts will make your job easier. Your students will understand the progression of your lecture and they will be able to focus on learning.

For more complicated lectures, I give my high school students an outline of my lecture with key words blanked out. Students fill in the blanks as they listen to the lecture. The task of filling in the blanks keeps the students focused. At the end of the lesson, students often help one another fill in the few blanks they missed during the lecture.

Models

Abstract concepts are easily forgotten unless they are put in real-life contexts. Teachers often use *models* to bridge the gap between abstract concepts in the lesson and the world beyond the classroom. Models are examples, demonstrations, descriptions, and analogies of things or ideas that cannot be readily observed. Effective models usually draw from the life experiences of the student. Models are also memorable.

Cognitively, students use models in different ways. Some students have no trouble understanding abstract concepts and can think of many examples. These students use the models to check their understanding of the concept. Other students remember the model better than they remember the concept and will use the model to reconstruct their knowledge of the concept. In both cases, the model is an effective tool for teaching and learning.

I suggest you use models (that is, demonstrations, examples, and verbal descriptions) in your instruction frequently. Models, frankly, make your lectures memorable. If you want your students to remember what you said—the objective of a lecture—then illustrate each abstract concept you present and give a real-life example for every major point of your lecture. (Chapter 8, "Models: The Memorable Part of the Lesson," will explain the art of modeling concepts.)

Check for Understanding

Unfortunately, most students have blank expressions on their faces while listening or concentrating. While I lecture, I wonder if the students are following what I say. At times, I worry that I am boring them, especially if I do not find the material particularly interesting. Over the years, I have become better at reading students' body language. Active note-taking usually indicates a high level of interest; closed eyes and a dropped head mean that I am not reaching that student. As a lecturer, I need feedback to know if the students understand or not. I check for understanding.

To check for understanding, I ask questions and have students signal answers. For example, I will ask a multiple-choice question that requires students to apply some information or concept I just presented. I give three possible answers. The students discreetly signal their answers with one, two, or three fingers on their upper chest where only I can see it. In a matter of seconds, I know what proportion of the class understands. I can make an informed decision to move on or review. Sometimes, I take a poll; I ask students to signal me if they want me to spend more time on the topic I am presenting. Students signal thumbs up for yes, thumbs to the side for neutral, and thumbs down for no. Again, within a matter of seconds, I know how to continue. (See sidebar 7.1 for another signal.)

One technique I find effective to check for understanding of the entire class is to ask a question. I request that all the students in the class write the answer in their notes. While they are writing, I circulate through the room and read their answers. I can easily tell who understands and who does not. Then, I select a student with a correct answer to answer the question. I continue by calling on students who have correct answers but different approaches to the question. I like this technique because I learn a great deal about what my students' understand, their creativity, their original ideas, their errors, and their misconceptions. I avoid calling on students with incorrect answers so misinformation does not creep into my lecture. This method also avoids potential embarrassment to students with wrong answers.

Student Note Taking

One of my maxims for teaching is: *if you want it in their notes, write it on the board*. Students must make decisions while listening to a lecture. They must decide if what you are saying is something they will need to study for the exam or if it is worth remembering. Sometimes teacher and student have different notions of what is important.

It confounds me to see my students busily taking notes on an interesting but unimportant aside and then find no one taking notes a few minutes later while I am delivering the most important part of my lecture. I have been known to redirect my students' efforts. I interject, "You do not need to take notes on this," or "This is important; put it in your notes!" This last declaration creates intense activity. I try to keep a positive perspective and remember that for students, it is not easy to distinguish the relative significance of different parts of a lecture.

The best way to ensure that the important points of your lecture are in the students' notes is to write the points on the board. I have noticed that when a teacher picks up the chalk to write on the board, the students poise their pencils to take notes. What the instructor writes on the board, the students write in their notes. (In chapter 12, "Working with Visual Aids," I describe how to use an overhead projector, PowerPoint presentations, and chalkboard effectively.)

SIDEBAR 7.1 Clueless

One physics teacher taught me the universal symbol of clueless. If students are not following your lesson and are too embarrassed to say so, they can send you the clueless signal. They form a C with their fingers and place it on their forehead. This can be casually done by (1) placing the elbow on the desk and by slouching the head to meet the hand or (2) pretending to stretch with bent elbows and one hand against the forehead. The lecturer can easily see the signal from the front of the room, but the signal is not obvious from the seats. This simple gesture provides valuable feedback to the teacher, who can then stop for questions, repeat difficult information, ask students to point out ambiguities, etc.

Another way that I assist student note taking is to create an outline of my lecture and leave blanks in it for students to fill in important information. That way the students receive the information that I think is important; however, I do not give them all of the information to assure that they stay attentive and hear the information they need to complete the notes. An outline of lecture notes is easy to generate, especially if I am lecturing from a PowerPoint file. I click on normal view, which has the text for each of the frames listed on the left side of the screen. I "select all" the text for the lecture and copy it; then I paste it into a word processing document. Next, I clean up the document and substitute a line for key words the students need to fill in from listening to the lecture. The students appreciate these notes; they feel less anxious about taking notes and perhaps missing key points or facts.

Some readers may worry that if we give students outlines of lecture notes, we may not be preparing them for note taking in postsecondary education. However, the times and study skills are changing. Many professors at universities are now distributing their PowerPoint presentations to their students via course Web sites and e-mail messages. Students arrive in class with printouts of the presentations and write additional notes on them. High school students should experience this before moving on to postsecondary education.

Summaries

As I discussed in chapter 5, "Great Beginnings and Endings," summaries are important. In a traditional lecture, the speaker recaps the major points. I will not belabor this point; just remember: Tell them what you told them.

Attention Spans

American students have short attention spans. The traditional fifty-minute class is much longer than the average attention span. Generally, student attention rises to a peak about five minutes into a lecture; it falls away after twenty minutes and rises again at the end of the lecture.

In chapter 5, I wrote about the importance of using your first and last minutes of class wisely. Given what we know about adolescent attention spans, I suggest you consider dividing your class into three parts, especially if you teach on a block schedule (see sidebar 7.2). For example, if you are in a lecture mode you could deliver two mini-lectures with an intervening activity, such as a student discussion, a slide presentation, or a problem-solving activity. If you sense your class is not attentive while you are delivering a longer lecture, take a break, such as asking the class to stand up and stretch, or tell a joke. Taking one or two

Sidebar 7.2 Planning for Block Scheduling

Many schools across the country are using block scheduling, with seventy-five to ninety-minute periods rather than the standard forty-five to fifty-five–minute period. The students have four classes per day. I have taught on a block schedule and a standard schedule. Block scheduling requires more variety in instruction to hold the students' attention. For a block, I tried to plan three or four different activities each day. For example, I gave a lecture with a PowerPoint presentation on planetary orbits, students read their textbook and answered questions, and then students used golf balls and a light to experience phases of the moon and drew what they observed. I found that requiring one assignment per day kept students on task. The activities shifted between teacher-centered to student-centered. I found that the variety keeps students engaged in learning. When students are engaged in learning, fewer discipline problems occur.

minutes for a diversionary activity will be worth the investment of time to get your students back into the learning mode.

Performing

A good lecturer is part actor. For example, good lecturers project both their voices and their personalities. They gesture to reinforce their words, walk around the room, and engage students with eye contact. They vary their paces—slowing for important points and moving more quickly for asides and illustrations. Good lecturers "read" their audiences and modify their lectures according to audience response. For example, if students are too busy taking notes to listen to the next point, the lecturer slows the delivery.

The image of the knowledgeable teacher standing behind a podium in the front of a classroom lecturing from bell to bell is passé. Today, students of all ages are exposed to mass media. They are accustomed to high-quality productions with good actors, music, and graphics that entertain and hold their attention. Media specialists are aware of people's attention spans and sensory preferences and use this knowledge to their advantage rather than ignoring it, like so many academics do. Teachers can successfully compete with the media. Think of yourself as giving a live performance. Even with all the media entertainment available, live performances are still quite popular. Students appreciate teachers who try to make lectures engaging as well as informative. (See chapter 6, "Instructional Strategies and Techniques," storytelling section.)

Consider storytelling as part of your repertoire of teaching strategies. People of all ages like listening to storytellers. After I learned that one of my world geography classes comprised primarily auditory learners, I changed my teaching technique to include storytelling. I began to tell what places looked, sounded, and smelled like and what I ate while I was there. I talked about my experiences getting off the airplane and traveling in foreign lands and my impressions during my travels. The students were far more attentive than if I lectured about national dress, customs, food, or transportation.

So, as they say in showbiz for good luck in a performance: Break a leg.

Sidebar 7.3 Tips for a Good Lecture

Before the Lecture

(1) Concentrate on developing a framework of concepts and relate them to one another, to past learning, and to future learning. Do not pack your lecture full of facts and details. Your students can get these from the accompanying textbook or readings.

(2) Practice your lecture, especially if you are a novice. Practice helps the sentences and technical vocabulary flow during performance. The majority of us are not accustomed to talking nonstop for fifteen to thirty minutes; we must get accustomed to it. Also, practicing allows you to time your lecture. On paper, your lecture may seem short, but when you start talking it tends to balloon.

(3) Have your lesson plan, transparencies, maps, and so forth together in a folder or notebook.

During the Lecture

(4) Begin by capturing the students' attention with something related to the topic on which you will lecture.

(5) State the objectives and purpose of the lecture.

(6) Relate concepts you will cover to students' experiences and daily life.

(7) Use language that is clear and unambiguous to students. If you want to expand student vocabulary, explain the definitions of the words you are using. It does little good to lecture using words your students cannot understand.

(8) Break up the monotony of a lecture by varying pace and activities.

(9) Give students the opportunity to ask questions.

(10) Relate the concepts you are covering to one another, to the whole topic, and to concepts in previous lectures.

(11) Express your enthusiasm for the subject.

(12) Observe students' body language and facial expressions and respond to them.

(13) If the attention of your class drifts, take a break (for example, stand up, stretch, and breathe deeply).

(14) If you use videos or other audio-visual equipment, test it before class to make sure it is working. Position videos at the exact point you want to begin showing them and adjust the sound to the proper level. Make sure illustrations (for example, overhead transparencies or PowerPoint images) are readable from all parts of the room.

(15) Give a summary and describe how the concepts taught are related to the next lecture.

After the Lecture

(16) Write remarks in the margin of your lecture notes to remind yourself to improve troublesome sections.

Summary

To create a lecture that is easily understood and memorable, remember to:

- Write a framework of major and supporting concepts;
- Organize your lecture around this framework;
- Explain the interrelationships between concepts;
- Explain the structure and flow of your lecture to the audience;
- Use models (for example, demonstrations, descriptions, and illustrations) of abstract concepts;
- Check student understanding as you lecture;
- Help students take notes—if you want it in notes, write it on the board; and
- Summarize the major points of your lecture.

ONLINE RESOURCE

About.com: Secondary School. Lecture Pros and Cons. http://712educators.about.com/od/lessonplans/p/lecture.htm (accessed January 10, 2009).

Chapter 8

Models: The Memorable Part of the Lesson

Have you ever listened to a detailed and complex description of an object or process, only to feel confused and frustrated? You probably felt like blurting out, "Just show me!" You knew instinctively that the long description would become clear if the instructor would show you or demonstrate what s/he was describing. These instincts point to a powerful teaching tool: *models.*

The axiom "a picture is worth a thousand words" is especially applicable in the classroom. Good demonstrations, examples, and pictures are worth dozens of words, and they are definitely worth class time. Effective teachers use models often. A model is an example of an abstract concept, idea, principle, rule, generalization, or object that cannot be readily observed. For younger students, *concrete models*—examples they can perceive directly in the classroom—are best. For example, you can demonstrate that a magnet picks up an iron nail but not an aluminum can. A picture of a gnu and a recording of an African musical instrument provide clarity to descriptions of things not in the everyday experience of adolescents. For older students, analogies, recalling experiences, and verbal descriptions are also appropriate. Seeing, hearing, and feeling examples can greatly assist the learning process for students of all ages.

Often, students recall the model more easily than the underlying principle. Sometimes I use games or simulations to teach principles such as carrying capacity, habitat destruction, migration, and sustainable resource management. Sometimes students recall the games I teach and then reconstruct the principles from their memory of the game. New teachers are surprised and occasionally taken aback that some students recall how they learned the concept before they remember the concept. Most experienced instructors do not care which the student recalls first—what they learned or how they learned it. In either case, the student reflects and remembers the important part—the concept. I can better recall science principles that I have seen demonstrated than those I learned through listening to a lecture or that I read in a book. The clarity and reinforcement provided by models and demonstrations help many students learn better.

I like to use models because they give real-life examples of abstract ideas. Examples from the students' lives make learning relevant. Chemistry is full of abstract concepts that seem invisible because they happen at the atomic level. Diffusion is a good example. Diffusion is defined by *Webster's Tenth New Collegiate Dictionary* as "the process whereby particles of liquids, gases, or solids intermingle as the result of their spontaneous movement caused by thermal agitation and in dissolved substances move from a region of higher to one of lower concentration." To help students understand what that means, I give them two concrete examples. I place a saucer of a pungent liquid, such as a pine-scented household cleaner, in the front of the room. As students can identify the scent, I have them raise their hands. The students in the first row raise their hands before those in the back row. Then we discuss the definition and the example. I also use a drop of food coloring in a pan of water to demonstrate movement from high to low concentrations. I also like models because they teach through the senses other than hearing.

Guidelines for Using Models

Like other instructional techniques, models can work well or poorly. Here are five guidelines to help you use models effectively.

(1) Use models to highlight important characteristics or principles.

Models make lasting impressions, so choose one or more that clearly and unambiguously illustrate the most important characteristic of your principle. As you display the model, point out exactly what you want the students to notice. Your model may be obvious to you, but it may not be obvious to the students.

I recall one teaching session in which the teacher used a good model but did not emphasize or make clear the important points of the model. As a result, the model and the lesson were unsuccessful. In this model, a father was attempting to teach his young son to float on his back. After several unsuccessful attempts to float, the father enlisted the mother's assistance to model how to float. The father said to the child, "Look at your mom float." The child did; he saw her floating effortlessly. Perhaps he thought it was miraculous that she could float and he could not. I know from watching his later attempts that he did not learn anything useful about body position or relaxation from the mother's demonstration. The whole teaching/learning situation could have been improved if the father had said, "See how your mom's hipbones are pushed to the surface of the water? Look at her chin pointing to the sky, not toward her chest. The position of her hips and chin helps her float." These simple sentences would have drawn the child's attention to the most critical body positions necessary for floating. By providing this information, both the father and the child would have been more successful in their respective teaching and learning endeavors.

(2) Start simple, then move to the complex.

Maxim: learning the simple is easier than learning the complex. Corollary: learning the simple makes learning the complex easier. Applying this maxim and corollary to using models will help your students learn everything from the simple to the complex. For example, if you are demonstrating the use of commas in a series, you could use this sentence as a model: Sue purchased bananas, oranges, and apples. In this model, a comma is placed after each word in the series. A more complex example is: Sue purchased color, black and white, and slide film. The former example should be used first to unambiguously illustrate the use of commas. The latter, which could confuse the beginner, should be introduced only after students have shown mastery of the comma in the simpler series.

The world around us is filled with models, many of them complex. Finding simple models is difficult, but worth the search. Science education is a discipline that abounds with good examples of both simple and complex models. Textbook manufacturers routinely introduce simple models before the complex. For example, in many science textbooks, children learn about the parts of a flower from a simple cutaway diagram of a flower. The petals, stamen, pistil, and ovary are all clearly indicated and labeled. The teachers' edition then instructs the teacher to bring a variety of flowers, both simple and compound, into the classroom. Going from the diagram to the real-world object can be a bit of a shock. The parts so clearly labeled in the book often take different shapes and are difficult to see in a real flower. In compound flowers, the parts are often so minuscule that a magnifying glass and a certain degree of knowledge are necessary to identify the parts. Starting with a compound flower can be discouraging to novice botanists; however, a simple progression of models from simple to complex leads a learner to success.

(3) Plan and practice your models.

Choosing a good model or example takes forethought and planning. I prefer to select examples and models while writing my lesson plan. By planning the models ahead, I can also practice them before I use them in class; this ensures success. As an instructor, I find it embarrassing to repeatedly try a demonstration and have it flop. As a student, I grow impatient as a red-faced instructor wastes my time trying to make a demonstration work, while muttering, "This should do it; it worked for my colleague last week."

Demonstrations are like recipes—to make them turn out right, you have to tinker with them. Floating a paper clip on a glass of water is one of my favorite demonstrations of surface tension. The first time I saw a paper clip float, a seven-year-old child with tiny, dexterous fingers simply placed the paper clip on the water. It looked easy; I thought I would use it as a demonstration in my class. When I tried to float a paper clip, it sank. Soon I had a half-dozen clips at the bottom of the glass of water. I was frustrated by my inability, but greatly relieved that I had taken the time to practice this "simple" demonstration before attempting it in class. With experimentation, I found that if I filled a glass to the rim, I could launch the paper clip like a boat. I also found that I could create an L-shaped "stretcher" from one paper clip and use it to gently lower another onto the surface of the water. When I taught the class on the adhesion and cohesion of water, I floated my paper clip on the surface on my first attempt. Fortunately, I averted frustration through practice.

When practicing a model, give some thought to the students' perspective. Will the students be able to see the model? Is it big enough? Is it high enough so that students in the back rows can see it over the heads of those in the front rows? Does the action happen slowly enough for the students to grasp what is happening? Are you standing so that your body does not block the view of some of the students? If you answer no to any of these questions, you need to change something. The solution may be simple, such as bringing a small box to class to raise your model so everyone can see it. If your model is small you can carry it to various locations in the classroom and repeat the demonstration. If the action happens quickly, repeat the model several times so the students can see it.

(4) Accurate models reduce misinformation.

Learning correct information the first time is easier than: learning misinformation, figuring out something is wrong, understanding why it is wrong, discarding the misinformation, and then learning the correct information. As students begin to learn new material, they are subject to misinterpretations and misimpressions. Therefore, it is important that students receive precise information and that the accompanying models are accurate.

In the early stages of learning, I suggest that you create the models rather than let your students create them. Student models often are only partially correct and can start misimpressions among other students. I am not recommending that you exclude the students from offering models in discussion, but that you postpone their contributions. For example, students can offer examples after you have taught the concepts and given your model; you can then mentally evaluate the students' examples to check for their understanding of the subject. Positively reinforce students who give examples that involve the concept you taught. Ask for further explanation from students whose models do not appear to fit the concepts you taught. You might need to use "wrong answer" techniques to make sure that other students do not formulate misconceptions (see chapter 9, "Asking Questions").

(5) Teach generalizations first, exceptions second.

It seems that every rule has an exception; however, modeling the exception first is confusing. I suggest you use several examples of the rule first and save a model of the exception for later in the lesson. For example, if you are teaching a spelling class on forming plurals, you could demonstrate how most singular nouns become plural with the addition of *s* or *es*; however, some nouns indicate plural status without a final *s* (for example, I cut my hair yesterday). Most likely, you will not have to mention the exception. One or more of your students will mention it; they love to find examples that break the rules.

A word of caution: use non-controversial topics when creating models, if possible. Controversial topics can awaken emotions that can distract the learner from the lesson. Political and ethical topics can turn a simple grammar lesson into a raging debate that will thwart your efforts to teach grammar.

Here are some examples of memorable models that my students created. One biology student teacher created a square dance for cell division. In the dance, the chromosomes paired at the midline and slid down the spindles to the poles. A second student teacher demonstrated how a snake sheds its skin inside out by pulling his arm out of a sock. Another illustrated DNA replication using heavy-duty zippers twisted into a double helix. One of the student teachers demonstrated the polarity of water molecules by bending a stream of water falling from a faucet with a plastic rod charged with static electricity. Another student showed how oil spills on water bodies are cleaned up. He floated a pool of vegetable oil on a bowl of water. Then, he placed one drop of detergent on the oil. The oil instantly flowed away from the detergent and to the side of the bowl. He explained that an oil skimmer then scoops up the oil. In all of these cases, the model riveted the audience's attention on the lesson. The lessons were memorable, precise, and anything but boring.

For younger students, concrete models that they can see and touch are important. For older students who are capable of abstract thought, intangible models are also appropriate, and descriptions can help them recall experiences. In chapter 7, I recommend giving real-life examples for every major point in a lecture. I must admit that I do not drag props with me to do a concrete demonstration for each major point I make in a forty-five–minute lecture. However, I do use experiences from my own life to talk about events that are common to everyone. For example, in earth science, to illustrate pool and riffle sequences in streams, I describe floating down a river in an inner tube when I was a child. We bumped and bobbed through the shallow riffles and floated lazily in the deeper pools. To illustrate the soil erosion that occurs on non-vegetated slopes, I describe the muddy runoff from home construction sites after a thundershower. I use poems or paragraphs from books describing places, events, and reactions to those events. I also use examples from classic and recent movies and popular television shows. In each of these cases, I try to paint a verbal picture that makes the abstract concept real to the students.

Concrete models are also appropriate for older students. Demonstrations, maps, slides, charts, graphs, and diagrams enhance any lecture. For example, to illustrate landforms not found in the locality where I am teaching, I show pictures I took on vacation or photographs from *National Geographic* or the United States Geological Survey Web site; I use big wall maps to point out places I talk about. (Geographic literacy is low in the United States, so I point out places that everyone should know—Chicago and Germany—as well as more obscure places.) If you do not have a big wall map, you can make an overhead transparency from a newspaper or download a map from the Internet. Remember to write the source of the map on the overhead to give credit to the publisher. I also use charts and graphs of data that illustrate trends I am talking about.

One of my favorite courses in my freshman year at college was a combined physics/chemistry class in which the instructor performed a demonstration each day. He showed us the height mercury rises to in a column; that electrical current creates a magnetic field and deflects a compass needle; that gravity acts on an object in horizontal flight at the same rate that it acts on a falling object. In one of my favorite courses in my senior year, the instructor showed slides daily to illustrate his lectures about places that were too far away for us to visit. Creating demonstrations and sorting slides took extra preparation time for these professors; however, the payoff was big—their students remembered what they were taught. Decades later, I remember the content of these classes better than I recall the content of lectures in which the professor did not bother to use models.

I also like to use models because they give me the opportunity to introduce a little humor into the classroom. For example, when I teach evapotranspiration, I take a long string of large toy pop beads and put them in an equally long cardboard tube. I explain that the cardboard tube is analogous to xylem, the tubes in a tree that carry water; the beads represent molecules of water. Then, I begin my lecture, drawing diagrams of a tree and the location of xylem. I go on to describe the process. As one molecule of water evaporates from the leaf—escapes into the air as water vapor—it pulls the next molecule up to the leaf surface. To simulate evaporation, I pluck a bead from the tube and toss it into the air. With a straight face, I continue to explain that as the temperature increases, so does the rate of evaporation. Accordingly, I snatch the beads from the tube and toss them into the air with increasing rapidity—colorful beads fly everywhere. The students stare, amazed and amused. A little humor goes a long way toward nurturing student goodwill. If I introduce humor occasionally, students are more willing to patiently endure the times my class is boring.

All teachers hope their lessons are clear and memorable. It is my dream to have the entire class remember, with clarity, the major points of my lectures and lessons. You, too, can make great strides toward this goal by using models. The next time your students have puzzled looks on their faces when you present an abstract concept, give them a concrete model. You will know your model has been successful when your students exclaim, "Now, I get it!" Or "Oh, I see!"

Summary

Good demonstrations, examples, and pictures are worth dozens of words. Effective teachers use models often to illustrate abstract concepts. Here are five guidelines for using models:

- Use models to highlight the most important characteristic or principle;
- Start simple then move to the complex;
- Plan and practice your models;
- Use exact models first so you do not have to spend time correcting false impressions; and
- Teach generalizations first, exceptions last.

Models are worth the effort and time it takes to create them. Models make your lessons memorable.

ONLINE RESOURCES

About.com: Secondary Education. Demonstrations & Experiments. http://chemistry.about.com/od/demonstrationsexperiments/Demonstrations_Experiments.htm (accessed January 10, 2009).

Apple Learning Interchange. Opening Classroom Doors. Teaching methods. Demonstrations. http://newali.apple.com/ali_sites/ali/exhibits/1000328/Demonstrations.html (accessed January 10, 2009).

Chapter 9

Asking Questions

Asking questions is an essential part of teaching. Asking questions is also central to good learning. One study revealed that new teachers ask roughly one question per minute. Another showed that 80 percent of classroom talk centers on asking, answering, and reacting to questions. Anything teachers do that often should be done well.

Requesting that students answer questions is a great way to move students out of passive learning into active learning. Passive learners absorb what they are taught. They often sit and listen. "You teach me" is their maxim. Active learners participate more fully in the learning process. They ask and answer questions, interact with new information, and respond with ideas of their own. Active learners engage with the material presented. Helping students make the transition from passive to active learning requires a skillful teacher. The teaching objective is to move passive students beyond simply restating what you have told them to pulling ideas together and drawing conclusions.

In this chapter, you will gain insight into the difference between passive and active learning. You will learn nine techniques for using questions effectively in your classroom. You will also learn how to deal with wrong answers.

Examine the Intent and Purpose of Your Questions

To examine your use of questions in the classroom, you need to distinguish between two types of questions: procedural and content. Procedural questions are those that deal with classroom routine (for example, Does everyone have their textbook? Who needs a worksheet?) Content questions are those that advance the lesson.

Early in their preparation to be teachers, I request that students write a purpose for each content question in their lesson plans. (If you recall, I include a list of questions in the instructional sequence section of my lesson plan.) The exercise is difficult. It makes the students ponder the intent and value of each question, and how individual questions fit into the set of questions, and what the set of questions accomplishes. At first, students tend to write questions that exercise recall skills. After seeing the word recall marching down the list of questions, they begin to change the kind and purpose of the questions. When they finish the assignment, their lessons include a variety of questions. The purposes often include: review, monitor comprehension, practice application of a formula, develop prediction and estimation skills, use analytical skills, practice skills used in assessment, and transfer knowledge from one situation to another. Usually, one use of this exercise is sufficient to make student teachers aware of the value of analyzing questions. With time, analyzing questions and question sets becomes an automatic, subconscious process.

I also request that student teachers analyze their sets of questions for progression of difficulty, logical order, and balance between convergent and divergent questions.

Questioning Techniques

The following is a description of nine techniques that will increase the effectiveness of asking questions in the classroom. I suggest you practice them the next time you teach a lesson. Remember, the techniques here are based on observation and research. The way you implement them is your artistic expression.

(1) After asking a question, wait three to five seconds before you call on a student to answer it.

This one technique alone will improve the quality and quantity of your students' responses. This short *wait time* produces near miraculous results. Your students produce more complex and longer answers. The wait promotes higher levels of thinking. More students are ready to answer the questions, not just the verbally quick and intuitive students. Also, increased wait time is helpful to English language learners.

To the new and nervous teacher, three seconds can seem like an eternity. To the enthusiastic teacher who has a discussion rolling, it may seem like a break in the momentum. I assure you, a three- to five-second wait will not damage your lesson; it will enhance it. Increasing your wait time to three to five seconds takes practice. I fall into the enthusiastic teacher category; I find myself increasing the pace of the class during discussions when the students are answering well; however, I know that to keep their answers of high quality, I have to let them think before talking. To use up some of my energy and keep the pace of the lesson slower, I stroll from one side of the room to the other between asking a question and requesting a specific student to answer. When I first started using this technique, I counted one–one hundred-thousand, two–one hundred-thousand, three–one hundred-thousand while I walked to make sure I was not rushing. The counting worked. After a few classes, I had established a wait time that I could maintain without counting.

(2) Call on non-volunteers as well as volunteers.

Before you use this technique, let your class know you are going to do it. When I mention this teaching tip to my classes of future teachers, they often object. I think the objections stem from the students' own anxieties about being called on when they do not know an answer. I prove to the class the necessity and validity of calling on non-volunteers by asking them two questions. First, I ask, "Why do students volunteer to answer questions?" They respond that students:

- know the answer;
- want to answer an easy question so they do not have to answer a hard question later;
- want credit for knowing the answer;
- want the teacher to know that they did their homework last night.

Then, I ask, "Why do students not volunteer to answer questions?" They respond that students:

- do not know the answer;
- are too shy to speak in class;
- have an attitude problem;
- did not do their homework last night.

Finally, I ask the students, "Which group of students (volunteers or non-volunteers) needs the teacher's help more?" With a look of "I get it" on their faces, my students agree that the non-volunteers need the teacher's help and that teachers should call on non-volunteers.

When calling on non-volunteers, do it primarily when the student knows the answer or can be prompted into giving the correct answer. In the beginning, you may want to call on non-volunteers to give opinion answers, or when no correct answer is needed. For example, in geography class, when calculating linear distance using a scale, you might ask shy students where in North America they would like to visit. Then, use the example to calculate the distance. This way you are helping students to feel more confident in their ability to contribute to class work. As their confidence builds, you can ask more academically challenging questions.

(3) Re-question students already called on.

Students are more attentive in class if they know they can be called on at any time. Occasionally, I see students falling asleep in class once they have given their answer for the day. Students are responsible for being active learners throughout your entire class.

(4) Ask for clarification.

Teachers tend to assume students know complete answers if the students can give partial answers. Teachers also tend to assume students know why an answer is correct. I recommend you do not complete students' partial answers or explain them. Instead, prompt them for a more complete answer. To prompt for further response, you can say something encouraging, like "good, can you expand on that?" You will gain more insight into what your students are learning if you let them do the talking.

(5) Ask questions of all your students.

Do not establish a pattern of calling on students in one location. It is easy to call on students in your immediate line of sight—the front row and down the middle of class. After teaching for about a semester and a half, I noticed that I asked fewer questions of the students in the front right corner of class. I often step to the left of the chalkboard after writing. With the slight angle of my shoulders, the students in the right corner were only in my peripheral vision. To remedy this situation, I periodically change sides of the chalkboard or stand with my back flat against the chalkboard.

One technique to identify your biases is to create a seating chart of the class; every time you call on someone, put a mark on the chart in that student's location. At the end of class, analyze your chart for patterns and equitable treatment of students.

Self-awareness is the key to identifying and changing habits that prevent you from being equitable to all your students.

(6) Increase the complexity of your questions.

As class progresses, you should increase the difficulty of your questions. At the beginning of class, you may ask a few questions that require students to recall information from your last lecture or their reading. The easy, recall questions will serve as a review, move the students into the topic for the day, and raise their confidence. As class time proceeds, you can increase the difficulty of the questions. This technique may seem too simple. I mention it, however, because I have seen teachers start out their class on such a difficult level that students retreat into passive-learning mode and refuse to answer questions. (In the next chapter, "Little Thoughts and Big Thoughts," I describe higher- and lower-order thinking skills and Bloom's taxonomy. This information will help you create easier and more demanding questions for your students.)

(7) Develop questions that help transfer knowledge to new situations or topics.

Transferring knowledge from one context to another is an advanced thinking skill. Teachers help students transfer knowledge by giving and asking for examples and developing questions around those examples. For example, if you are discussing gas laws, you can lead the students through a series of questions on how a refrigerator works and why mountaintops are cooler than valleys. If you are teaching solubility and temperature, you could ask questions about the difference between dissolving sugar in hot tea versus iced tea. In many cases, helping students transfer knowledge is a matter of finding real-life applications for theory and asking questions about these applications.

(8) Prompt students to give more-complete answers.

When a student responds to a question with "I don't know" or gives a weak answer, a partially incorrect answer, or an incorrect answer, I ask other questions. This process helps the student form or improve an answer. Teachers often have a sense that a correct answer is hidden behind student shyness, or that with a little clarification, the confusion obscuring a student's answer will disappear. In these cases, you can help your students develop their response by asking *convergent questions* (that is, specific questions that point the student toward the answer). For example,

> *Teacher:* What sources of pollution exist in our community?
>
> *Student:* I don't know.
>
> *Teacher:* Look out the window. Do you see a clear blue sky?
>
> *Student:* No, it's smoggy.
>
> *Teacher:* What causes the smog?
>
> *Student:* Junk in the air.

Teacher: OK. Do you recall the discussion yesterday about electrical generation and transportation in which we discussed where that junk comes from?

Student: Oh yeah, burning coal to produce energy, plus cars and trucks, create a bunch of stuff, like carbon dioxide and nitrous oxide.

Teacher: Good job!

(9) Redirect questions to hear a variety of responses.

To redirect a question, ask a question and then call on several students without restating or rephrasing the question. This redirection technique elicits multiple answers for an opinion question or explores options when there are several correct answers. In this technique, the teacher asks a question, waits for three seconds, and calls on a succession of students. For example,

> *Teacher:* "At what age do you think sex education should start in public school?" (pause) Ted?
>
> *Ted:* Kindergarten.
>
> *Teacher:* Mary?
>
> *Mary:* Never, sex education should be taught at home.
>
> *Teacher:* Steve?
>
> *Steve:* Twelve.
>
> *Teacher:* Susan?
>
> *Susan:* Second grade.
>
> *Teacher:* We heard a variety of responses, ranging from kindergarten to age twelve and one never.

In the dialogue above, notice how the teacher did not rephrase the question. The first time I use the re-questioning technique in class, I describe it to my students, and warn them that I am not going to repeat the question. About halfway through, a student comes out of a fog and asks, "What's going on?" I smile, and the students around him/her explain. The lesson continues.

I also use the technique to review. For example, the class meeting after explaining and using the requestioning technique, I start the class by asking a general question about the topic of the lesson (for example, name or describe a characteristic of gas giant planets that we covered in lecture and reading on Tuesday). A few hands go up and the remaining students dive for their notes. I call on volunteers to begin with and then non-volunteers. The students review the previous lesson and I listen.

I like the redirection technique because it gives me insight into student thinking in a short period of time.

Handling Incorrect Responses

Teaching the correct information the first time is easier than correcting misinformation. To teach new information, you have to introduce it to students and let them interact with it multiple times before they learn it. To correct something that is learned incorrectly is a multiple-step process. First, you have to identify the misconception. Then, you have to explain why it is wrong. Next, you teach the new learning; and finally, you reinforce the new learning. What a process! Prevention is easier than remediation.

Try to be alert to misinformation coming into your class. If you think a student is going to give the wrong answer, avoid calling on him/her. If you do not know who has the correct answer, use one of the techniques for checking for understanding described in chapter 7, "Lecture, If You Must." One technique is to request that the students write an answer to a question in their notes. As they write, walk around the room surveying their notes for a correct answer.

If a student answers incorrectly, I suggest two things: (1) deal with the wrong answer immediately and (2) be kind. Contrary to my advice to start lessons with an example of the rule, not the exception, I am going to start this section with a negative example. Responding with a resounding "Wrong!" to an incorrect answer and moving on to another student embarrasses the first student. Embarrassment and ridicule hinder student participation. As teachers, we are to help students learn, not punish them. Learning is a process fraught with incorrect answers along the way. Teachers need to give students the freedom to make mistakes and to experiment within the learning process. By responding in an unkind or harsh manner to incorrect responses, teachers can extinguish the freedom to be wrong in the classroom. Ultimately, this limits learning.

Here are some phrases I have heard teachers use in response to wrong answers:

- Nice try, but that is not the answer I'm looking for;
- Good thinking, but that's not quite it;
- Almost (with an encouraging smile);
- Interesting answer, but I don't see how you got it;
- You have something there; Mary, help Tom complete that answer.

All of these responses reinforce the student's participation, but do not indicate the response is correct.

Listening to students' answers is difficult. New teachers often have an answer in mind and listen only for it. Sometimes, however, students come up with an answer that takes an entirely different approach than expected. Rather than rejecting these answers as wrong, we need to discuss them at some point during the lesson.

Madeline Hunter (1982) recommends the following process for correcting students. She says that when students give wrong answers, it demonstrates they do not know two things. First, they do not know the answer to the question you asked, and second, they do not know the question for the answer they gave. Hunter suggests that teachers ask a question, supply a prompt, ask again, and make the student accountable. Here is an example:

> *Teacher:* Who became the president of the United States after Abraham Lincoln was assassinated?
>
> *Student:* Andrew Jackson.
>
> *Teacher:* You are almost correct. If I had asked who was the seventh president, you would be right. Do you remember the senator also named Andrew, who lived in Greeneville, Tennessee, and whose last name also started with a J?
>
> *Student:* Andrew Johnson.
>
> *Teacher:* That's right. I expect you to remember that so you'll get it correct on the worksheet this afternoon.

Sometimes you will need to give the student two prompts. If the student still seems lost, move on to the next student. The first student will learn from the ensuing discussion.

Questions—a Tool for Classroom Control

Questions are a wonderful way of taking care of minor discipline problems in your classroom. You can call on talkers and daydreamers to answer questions, drawing them back into the lesson. In some segments of today's society, most students with behavioral problems in secondary classrooms are male. You may create a gender bias in your classroom if you call on students for discipline reasons. Be careful to ask females in the classroom an equal number of questions and questions of equal difficulty.

Summary

Asking questions is essential to teaching and learning. Questions help teachers monitor the students' understanding and thought processes. When writing lists of questions to include in your lesson, examine the intent and purpose of each question and the series of questions. Here are nine questioning techniques to help you be a more effective teacher:

- After asking a question, wait three to five seconds before you call on a student to answer it;
- Call on non-volunteers as well as volunteers;
- Re-question students already called on;
- Ask for clarification;
- Ask questions of all your students;
- Increase the complexity of your questions;
- Develop questions to help transfer knowledge to new situations or topics;
- Prompt students to give more-complete answers; and
- Redirect questions to hear a variety of responses.

Remember to respond to wrong answers immediately and kindly.

REFERENCES

Hunter, M. 1982. *Mastery Teaching*. El Segundo, Calif.: TIP Publications.

ONLINE RESOURCES

About.com. Secondary Education. Asking Better Questions with Bloom's Taxonomy. http://specialed.about.com/od/teacherchecklists/a/bloom.htm (accessed January 10, 2009).

Apple Learning Interchange. Teaching & Learning. Teaching Practice. Opening Classroom Doors. Teaching Methods. Questioning Techniques. http://newali. apple.com/ali_sites/ali/exhibits/1000328/Questioning_Techniques.html (accessed January 10, 2009).

Chapter 10

Little Thoughts and Big Thoughts

Much of education is introduced in small pieces. We ask students to: memorize this definition, recite that law, name that mountain range, read this and tell me what it said in your own words, or solve for x in the math problem $2x + 3 = 13$. Unfortunately, much of secondary education is based around such and requires *lower-order thinking skills*. Lower-order thinking skills include knowledge, comprehension, and application.

Asking lower-order thinking skill questions does have advantages. Questions for worksheets and tests are easy to construct and answers are easy to grade. However, life outside school rarely includes multiple-choice tests; adults often are evaluated on their abilities to do complex tasks. So why do we educate our children with simplified pieces? Is there a more effective method we can use?

Higher-order thinking skills include analysis, synthesis, and evaluation. These skills require students to pull together background information and then process the information to produce original thoughts. By original thoughts I mean original to the students. The thoughts of the students may be ideas that were published 150 years ago; however, if students have not been exposed to these ideas, I consider their answers original thoughts.

Today we talk of students constructing their own knowledge. For example, kindergartners discover that $1 + 2 = 2 + 1$. The joy of discovery shows on their faces. It is their discovery. They created the knowledge, and they own it. It is not important that the commutative property has been known for hundreds of years.

Bloom's Taxonomy

The following is a classification system to help you categorize questions and objectives according to the level of thought processes. *Bloom's taxonomy* is probably the best-known system for classifying questions and objectives. The taxonomy will give you a way of analyzing questions that you ask in class and learning objectives that you use in lesson plans. Bloom's taxonomy is useful for writing discussion questions, tests, and worksheets. It is also useful for analyzing the level of difficulty of questions in interactive lectures.

These categories progress in difficulty of thinking skills involved in answering the question or fulfilling the objective. The progression of lower-order thinking skills is knowledge, comprehension, and application. The progression of higher-order thinking skills is analysis, synthesis, and evaluation.

KNOWLEDGE

The first level of Bloom's taxonomy, *knowledge,* requires recall or recognition of information. The student is requested to recall what was learned; no further analysis or processing of the information is required. The student answers questions or performs tasks related to terminology and facts, conventions, classifications and categories, and methodology. The following tasks ask students to use knowledge skills:

- Define synapse.
- Name the continents.
- Who is the secretary general of the United Nations?
- What are the first three prime numbers?
- What are the physical and chemical properties of carbon?

Even though knowledge is the lowest level of the thinking skills, it forms the foundation for more advanced learning. We cannot ask students to use higher-level thinking skills if they have no background knowledge to use in their analysis. Our society requires people to memorize many things, such as traffic rules, the value of coins and currency, how to punctuate a sentence, and where to vote. A good citizen or parent needs to memorize substantial knowledge.

The problem is that some teachers substitute learning primarily in the knowledge realm for progressing their students to higher-order thinking. Information that is memorized and not interacted with in another form is soon forgotten. Memorization alone leads to superficial understanding of a topic. Do you remember my sign, "Naming ≠ Knowing"? Just because students can define the technical terms related to a topic does not mean they understand that topic. Without requesting that students do more than parrot what they have learned, you have no way of knowing if they understand the information.

COMPREHENSION

The second level of Bloom's taxonomy, *comprehension,* requires the student to organize or arrange the information or knowledge into other terms or another form of communication. At this level, the student must interact with the information in some way. Students are asked to interpret quotes, definitions, charts, graphs, and illustrations. In some cases, students must sort through a large amount of information to select what is pertinent. The following require students to exercise comprehension skills:

- What were the main ideas in yesterday's discussion?
- In your own words, define adiabatic lapse rate.
- Compare route A and route B on the map. Is route B shorter?
- On this graph, what happens to the temperature during the first five minutes?

Comprehension questions can be cued by such words and phrases as: in your own words, compare, contrast, rephrase, and condense. Comprehension questions can require little previous study or work (for example, what is the main idea of the first two lines of this essay?) or a tremendous amount of background knowledge (for example, read a music score; read an architectural plan; or translate a passage from one language to another).

APPLICATION

The third level of Bloom's taxonomy, *application,* requires students to apply previously learned information to new situations when no mode of solution is specified. The students select and use a rule, process, formula, and so forth, to arrive at a single correct answer. The situation must be new to the student or contain new elements compared with the situation in which the idea was learned. The following require students to use application skills:

- If oranges sell for $.50 and apples for $.30, how much would you pay for three oranges and two apples?
- Use the definition of longitude and latitude and a globe to determine the latitude and longitude of Knoxville, Tennessee.
- Calculate the area of these parallelograms.
- Which of the following five short poems is a limerick?
- If City A and City B are two inches apart on a map with a scale of 1:62,500, how many miles apart are they?

- To which kingdom, phylum, class, and order do monkeys belong? (Use the key provided to determine your answer.)

The ability to apply principles, generalizations, and rules to new situations is the springboard from which the remaining higher-order thinking skills are developed.

ANALYSIS

The fourth level of Bloom's taxonomy, *analysis,* is a higher-order thinking skill. Analysis questions require students to break something apart into components and understand how the components relate to one another and the whole. Students use analysis-level thinking to identify motives or causes, form conclusions, or find evidence to support or reject a hypothesis. These types of activities cause students to interact repeatedly with the information—categorizing, re-categorizing, and searching for clues or patterns. This repeated interaction helps students gain depth of understanding. The following require students to use analysis skills:

- Based on your observations of the campaign, why was candidate Jones elected?
- What evidence can you cite to support the generalization that matter expands when heated?
- From the following data, what conclusion can you draw?

Unlike application questions, analysis questions do not have a single correct answer. Analysis questions take time to answer; they require students to review what they know and put it together in new forms. This process takes time—often longer than the recommended three- to five-second wait time recommended for lower-order thinking skills question and answer sessions.

SYNTHESIS

The fifth level of Bloom's taxonomy, *synthesis,* requires students to think creatively. Students use synthesis skills to produce original communications (for example, write an essay, make a plan, or solve problems). To do these tasks, they must pull together elements to form a whole. Like analysis questions, synthesis questions take time to answer. Students must have a good understanding of the topic before being able to formulate sound plans, solve problems, or create original communications. The students must draw from previous knowledge to create their answer or product. The following require students to use synthesis skills:

- Design your own experiment to illustrate the gas laws.
- How can we indirectly measure the height of the building?
- How could you feed yourself if you lived at the seashore two hundred years ago?
- What would the United States be like if we had not won the Revolutionary War?
- Write a letter to your city council representative on the issue of drug use among adolescents.
- Write an essay or poem to express your feelings about the referendum on the ballot.

EVALUATION

The sixth level of Bloom's taxonomy, *evaluation,* involves the previous five levels of thinking. Evaluation requires students to make judgments on the merit of an idea, problem, solution, or aesthetic work. The students create criteria of their own to judge or use criteria given to them. Evaluation is a complex process. It should not be confused with quick decisions, which fall into the opinion category, but are judgments that are the result of careful consideration of various aspects of the object, process, concepts, or solutions being evaluated. Evaluation takes time and results in an original work. Again, there is no single right answer.

In the following examples, students use evaluation skills:

- Would you prefer to use method A or method B to do the experiment? Explain your answer.
- Should our town build a garbage incinerator?
- Which is the most aesthetic picture from these artists of the Renaissance period?

CONTEXT

The level of a question depends on its context or if the student has encountered the material previously. A question asked in yesterday's lesson that requires comprehension skills (for example, distilling the major points from a reading assignment) would be a recall question requiring knowledge-level skills in today's review of yesterday's class.

It is not important that you classify all of your questions, assignments, or activities according to Bloom's taxonomy. It is important, however, that you recognize lower-order and higher-order thinking skills and that you balance their use in your classes. Students need to learn basic information and processes; they also need to use this information as a springboard to higher-order thinking skills. The higher-order thinking skills are the same as those that we read about in the popular press—critical thinking that is teaching our children how to THINK.

Improving Your Teaching through Use of Bloom's Taxonomy

You ask, "What can you do with this well-known taxonomy?" My answer is, I do not teach about teaching without it. In chapter 9, "Asking Questions," you read about increasing the difficulty of questions as class progresses. I use Bloom's taxonomy to classify questions I ask during my discussions and inter-active lectures. In each class, I start off with knowledge and comprehension questions and then move to questions that require higher-order thinking skills.

I have a chart that helps me analyze questions asked by student teachers (see table 10.1). I use the chart to identify questioning patterns during evaluations. Every time the student teacher asks a question, I classify it and mark the appropriate box according to thinking-skill level and minutes elapsed since the beginning of the lesson. I can visually track whether the difficulty of the questions progresses during the lesson. With advanced student teachers, I see

TABLE 10.1 Recording Level of Thinking Skills Involved in Answering a Question

	<10 minutes	10–19 min.	20–29 min.	30–39 min.	40–49 min.
Knowledge					
Comprehension					
Application					
Analysis					
Synthesis					
Evaluation					
Procedural[a]					

[a]A procedural question is one that is related to classroom management (for example, Does everyone have their book open to page 76? Who wants to take this note to the office?) rather than advancing the cognitive portion of the lesson.

a gradual progression from many knowledge and comprehension questions to fewer application questions and to one or two analysis and synthesis questions. Good higher-order thinking skill questions build on a foundation of knowledge. An entire lesson may be built around providing the foundation for one synthesis or evaluation question.

I also use Bloom's taxonomy to keep myself honest. I can get on a roll—my lecture seems to flow, discussions are lively, the students seem eager to learn—yet, I must be concerned with the quality of the teaching / learning experience. Are my students exercising valuable thinking skills that will help them in the future? Are my test questions requiring a wide range of thinking skills to answer? Do my discussions really stimulate thought or do students just create variations of what I said in lecture? Bloom's taxonomy helps me answer those questions. In chapter 1, "Twelve Years as a Student Do Not Prepare You to Be a Teacher," I mentioned developing self-analysis skills to help you reflect on your teaching and improve your technique. You can now add Bloom's taxonomy to your arsenal of self-analysis techniques.

In today's educational community, we know that we must prepare students for life in the twenty-first century. The information age that futurists predicted several decades ago engulfs our workplaces and homes. Information of all types is readily available on the Internet. To prepare students to work in the information age, we need to let them develop and exercise higher-order thinking skills so they can process, analyze, synthesize, and evaluate the available information. Changing from a curriculum based on lower-order thinking skills to one based on higher-order thinking skills is difficult, but with imagination and diligence we can rise to the challenge.

Summary

Much of education can be reduced to small pieces: memorize this and recite that. However, many jobs today and later in the twenty-first century will

TABLE 10.2 Lower-order and Higher-order Thinking Skills

Lower-order thinking skills	Higher-order thinking skills
Knowledge	Analysis
Comprehension	Synthesis
Application	Evaluation

require higher-order thinking skills. Although it is important to help students build a knowledge base using lower-order thinking skills, it is equally important to ask questions and create assignments that require students to exercise higher-order thinking skills using that knowledge base.

REFERENCES

Bloom, B. S., ed. 1956. *Taxonomy of Educational Objectives Handbook 1 Cognitive Domain*. New York: David McKay.

ONLINE RESOURCES

About.com. Secondary Education. Asking Better Questions with Bloom's Taxonomy. http://specialed.about.com/od/teacherchecklists/a/bloom.htm (accessed January 10, 2009).

The Higher Education Academy. Writing Learning Objectives Using Bloom's Taxonomy. http://www.ukcle.ac.uk/resources/reflection/table.html (accessed January 10, 2009).

Chapter 11

Discussions and Interactive Teaching

Students arrive in the classroom with a wide variety of life experiences that can enrich your class. You can structure these experiences into your lessons through discussions in which students provide the real-life interpretation of concepts you present.

These discussions can take a variety of forms. *Large-group* discussions involve the whole class; *small-group* discussions involve two to six students. Discussions can be teacher led, student led, or interactive. Choose the form that suits your lesson, your teaching style, and the needs of your students.

The traditional discussion is teacher led. The teacher asks a question, and a student answers it. Next, the teacher comments on the student's answer; then, another student is called on to add to the discussion. The verbal action alternates between students and teacher. The teacher stays in overt control of the discussion. This type of discussion is good for training your students to participate in discussions or dealing with sensitive topics that may become volatile. At the university level, I prefer that my students learn to discuss matters among themselves rather than through me. Getting to that point with a secondary class, however, takes a lot of effort on the part of the teacher.

Ideally, a discussion will flow from the teacher to the students and then among the students. The teacher observes the discussion constantly, stepping in occasionally to redirect or summarize. Though the teacher appears less active, s/he is busy monitoring the discussion, making a list of points that students make (and comparing it to the list of points included in the lesson plan), foreseeing potential difficulty, thinking of examples or related research, and formulating a summary. Is it not amazing how calm teachers appear while undertaking all this mental activity?

A discussion requires preparation, as do other instructional methods. Discussion can be built around a list of questions, a problem to solve, a plan to be made, or an activity to be completed. All of these should require verbal interchange among group members. Like other assignments, discussions should have teaching objectives. To prepare a lesson plan for a discussion, first write the objectives, then create a list of questions that will help reach the objectives. Next, write a list of all the concepts, ideas, or facts that you want to result from the discussion. Finally, select a method of closure for the discussion.

In your lesson plan, estimate the amount of time your students need to complete the lesson. Keep track of time, because it tends to slip away during lively discussions. (See sidebar 11.1.)

To prepare students for small-group discussions, the teacher describes the assignment and divides the class into groups. Consider making the discussion assignment first, perhaps by writing it on the board and then creating the groups. Sometimes students are too busy thinking about moving into their groups to remember the assignment. Then, when their group is settled, they

---

Sidebar 11.1 Tips for Good Discussions

(1) Let everyone have a chance to speak. Prevent the loquacious and verbally quick students from monopolizing the discussion or overwhelming the quiet students.

(2) Address all comments to the entire group by projecting your voice and by using eye contact with students in many locations around the room. Do not let the discussion between you and a student or between two students drift toward a private conversation.

(3) Ask students to speak loudly enough for the entire class to hear. Do not repeat student comments.

(4) Students should take notes on the discussion. Unfortunately, students come to class with the impression that they only take notes on what the teacher says. Students need to know that they can learn from their peers, which is as valuable as learning from the teacher.

(5) Discussions, like lectures and other instructional methods, need summaries. You can summarize the major points of the discussion or let the students do it. Requesting that students summarize the discussion from their notes will be incentive to take notes.

(6) Displays of temper or name calling have no place in a discussion. Students who get angry or call other participants unflattering names lose the privilege of participating.

fall into conversation because they lack an assignment. A written assignment prevents such a waste of class time.

Purposefully changing the composition of small groups frequently during a semester allows students to hear a variety of viewpoints. When assigning groups, make sure to mix students in terms of gender, ethnicity, and academic achievement. It would be easy, but not as educational, for students to work in small groups with similar opinions, personalities, or backgrounds. By assigning the groups according to students' birth months or last digits in their telephone numbers, the teacher can assure variety. To limit confusion that comes with moving students into small groups around the room, you can prepare a list of students in each small group and its location; then, put the list on the overhead projector. (See sidebar 11.2 for small-group discussion tips.)

During small-group discussions, you may prefer to walk around the room and listen to the various discussions. By listening, you can monitor the quality of the discussion, gain insights into the students' learning, gauge the amount of time required to complete the assignment, and keep students on task. After students have completed their assignments, they tend to continue talking about

---

SIDEBAR 11.2 Tips for Small-Group Discussions

(1) Assign places for each discussion group as you assign the groups (for example, group one meets in the back right corner of the room and group two in the front left corner). This minimizes the confusion and time it takes for students to move into their groups. I admit that I dislike wasted class time, and I do not want to squander it on nonlearning tasks.

(2) Place the discussion assignment or questions on the board or overhead projector. Students may forget the assignment while they are moving to their discussion group. The transparency serves as a reminder, and it frees you from having to repeat the assignment.

(3) During small-group discussions, walk around the class listening to the discussion. Your presence will help keep groups on task.

(4) Give students notice that the discussion is going to end in a short time (for example, a two-minute warning). This will allow them to finish or summarize.

(5) Make groups accountable for their work. For example, students should prepare to present the salient points from their discussion.

their own interests. The noise level can remain constant even though the assignment is finished, so do not use noise level as an indicator of assignment completion.

Interactive Teaching

Some teachers successfully combine lecture and discussion formats. The lesson flows from the teacher to and among the students and back to the teacher. For example, the teacher may present a few concepts. Then, s/he calls on students to give examples, reactions, or answers to questions. The lesson alternates between teacher-centered talk and student responses. This technique is called *interactive teaching.*

As with other teaching methods, the instructional sequence for interactive teaching is outlined in a lesson plan. Concepts are listed, along with questions, in sequential order.

Interactive teaching takes some practice, but new teachers can develop the technique in increments. Begin by interspersing one or two questions in a lecture. As your confidence builds, include more questions. Soon you will flow easily between lecturing and leading discussion. Interactive teaching has great advantages over lecturing. The students are active learners, and the teacher can monitor what the students do and do not understand.

Summary

Discussions seem deceptively simple to lead. It appears that students are doing all the work and the teacher is relaxing, but that is far from reality. For effective discussions, teachers:

- Plan discussions like they would any other type of lesson;
- Write the discussion assignment and list of concepts that should be covered during the discussion;
- Organize groups of students so that the composition will lead to successful discussions;
- Monitor the progress of the groups and the time;
- Prepare to join the discussion to clarify or redirect; and
- Plan a summary or closure.

Ideally, the discussion flows from the teacher to the students and among the students. Discussion questions interspersed in a lecture make teaching more interactive and students more active learners.

ONLINE RESOURCES

About.com: Secondary Education. Whole Group Discussion Pros and Cons. http://712educators.about.com/od/lessonplans/p/discussions.htm (accessed January 10, 2009).

Saskatoon Public Schools. Instructional Strategies Online. What Is Interactive Instruction? http://olc.spsd.sk.ca/DE/PD/instr/intera.html (accessed January 10, 2009).

Chapter 12

Working with Visual Aids

I attend many conferences, student presentations, and guest lectures. The most noticeable errors I find in presentation techniques concern the use of chalkboards, slides, images from overhead projector transparencies, and PowerPoint presentations. Presenters often turn their backs to the audience, speak to the whiteboard, make eye contact primarily with the projector, or become so involved with the images on the screen that they forget to address the audience. With a little self-awareness, you can avoid these common pitfalls.

I must admit, I hesitated to include this chapter in this book. My intention here is not to reduce the field of teacher preparation to offering simple or trivial teaching techniques. Schools of education are often criticized for teaching students how to erase the blackboard and keep a grade book. I do not want to advance the idea that schools of education promote trivial learning, but repeated observation of untrained teachers and presenters convinced me that there is a need to learn the proper techniques for using a whiteboard—or chalkboard—and overhead projector. It will take between five and twenty minutes to read this chapter. By reading the chapter and then experimenting with the skills and techniques described, you might become a better teacher or presenter for life, which in the long run seems like a wise investment of time.

Whiteboard Use

(1) Speak, then write on the board.

Unfortunately, the image of the absent-minded professor lecturing to the chalkboard, writing with one hand and erasing with the other, is a reality. Fortunately, it is easy to avoid finding yourself in this position. Common courtesy calls for facing people when you are speaking to them, so simply speak to the class, then turn to write on the board. It may take some conscious effort to speak first, then write, but after a few lessons it should become easier to remember.

The technique of speaking and then writing is based on more than courtesy; it is also based on research. We can talk faster than we write. By speaking first, we allow students to transfer what they heard from "sensory memory" to short-term memory. Writing on the board usually takes two to ten seconds. This short period may seem like dead time to the teacher; however, the students are processing information. By speaking then writing, the teacher does not give the student the opportunity to guess what is being written. Often, students guess wrong. The student then has to make a mental correction. Remember that it is more difficult to re-teach misinformation than to teach correct information the first time.

(2) Speak while facing the class.

When you explain material on a board, talk with your back to the board, gesturing with the arm closest to the illustration. For example, if you have a diagram of a tool on the board and wish to explain the function of each of its parts, step to the right and point to the parts with your left hand. If you cross over your body to gesture with your right hand you will find yourself facing the board and trying to talk over your shoulder to the class. It feels awkward and looks comical.

Often, speaking while writing on the board results from an urge to hurry. If you feel rushed, you are trying to pack too much material into one class session, or you have not budgeted your class time appropriately.

(3) Write Key Words, Simple Illustrations, Formulas.

Now that you know when and how to write on the board, let us address what to write on the board. In general, write key words and phrases. In chapter 7, "Lecture, If You Must," I mention the maxim, "If you want it in their notes, write it on the board." Typically, the things teachers want in student notes are major concepts, new vocabulary words, diagrams and illustrations, and assignments. Teachers write on the board to (1) reinforce student learning, (2) clarify ambiguities, (3) illustrate objects and processes not observable in the classroom, and (4) signal students that what is being explained is of greater value than other information presented but not written on the board. You can also use the board for clarification when you notice students are confused or if you anticipate that students may have trouble distinguishing between two words that sound similar. In this case, write both words on the board with their definitions.

(4) Where you put it matters.

Using the board haphazardly, and writing wherever space permits, is ineffective and confusing. Placement indicates the relationship or relative importance of words and concepts on the board. The following is a short description of three different placements of words and interpretation of their meaning.

(A) An outline form suggests a hierarchy of importance. For example,

I. Major concept

    A. Minor concept

    B. Minor concept

        1. Example of minor concept

The position of A and B indicate they are of similar importance, but less important than I. The 1 is subordinate and related to B.

(B) Writing words one below the other suggests sequencing. For example,

    January

    February

January comes before February. Numbering your list from the top down can indicate a sequence or diminishing importance.

(C) Side-by-side placement suggests equal value, parallel relationship, or oppositional relationship. For example,

    Advantages of Plan A   Advantages of Plan B

This side-by-side placement suggests equality and an oppositional relationship. The placement does not suggest one is more important than the other or that one came first.

Now that you are aware of the implications of position on the board, you can use placement to your advantage.

(5) Erase the board.

I have a colleague who is so enthusiastic about teaching physics that he only partially erases the board to write in a new formula. Sometimes he erases a small hole in a complicated problem to write a new formula. I have trouble distinguishing the old from the new. For students who are visual learners, his board must present a confusing and baffling mental image. Fortunately, there is a quick, simple fix to this problem: erase the board completely.

When you finish teaching one concept, erase the board before you present the new concept. Remember: New Concept = Clean Board.

Sometimes, I feel rushed and do not want to take the time to erase the board. One day, I timed myself erasing the board with a few key words on it. It took me four seconds. Another day, I timed myself erasing a board full of notes after group discussions. It took fourteen seconds. After I finished erasing the board, I asked my students if they were bored while I erased. They looked somewhat baffled and indicated they were not. They were busy processing the information from the discussion and did not notice the short time it took to erase the board. When I do not want to take the time to erase the board, it is a red flag to me. I realize that my haste is an indicator that I am rushing my lecture—not that I am wasting class time.

Overhead Projector Use

The guidelines given above also pertain to the use of an overhead projector. With an overhead projector, however, you must be sensitive to one additional factor. *When you turn out the lights, the students tend to go to sleep.* You need to make this part of your presentation more interesting to overcome the tranquilizing effect of dim light. The use of the overhead projector also presents other unique problems.

Although I like the convenience and ease of using the projector, its intense light temporarily blinds me. I have trouble seeing my class and making eye contact with the students after writing on the plastic film. To remedy this problem, I use previously prepared overheads. When I need to write extensively or repeatedly, I use the board.

Presenting complicated diagrams with prepared transparencies on the overhead projector is much easier and less time-consuming than trying to draw them on the board. In addition, many textbook companies sell overhead transparencies to accompany their textbooks.

Here are a few tips for using the overhead projector. Like most of my tips, they come from repeated observations of new teachers making mistakes.

(1) Point to the image on the screen, not the transparency on the projector.

By standing with your back to the screen and gesturing with the inside arm, you can maintain eye contact with your audience. Pointing to the screen ensures that your body does not obstruct the image; you also avoid creating large hand shadows. By standing next to the screen, you also do not block the students' view.

(2) Teach the students, not the projector.

Sometimes new teachers get so mesmerized by the bright light of the projector and by changing transparencies that they forget their audience. It is wise to do some self-analysis to see if you are making good eye contact with your students, speaking to them and not to the projector.

(3) Move around the classroom.

Remember, you are not tethered to the projector. Avoid the tendency to stand or sit immediately beside this piece of equipment.

(4) Prepare transparencies in advance.

Creating transparencies that you use regularly also makes teaching future classes easier. I make my own transparencies using a variety of software programs. By using prepared transparencies you do not have to copy definitions or formulas onto a board. You can place the prepared transparency on the projector and then move around the classroom to monitor student work and encourage appropriate behavior. (It is harder to fall asleep if your teacher is standing near you.) If your transparencies contain several points, you can choose to reveal them individually by covering the remainder with a partial sheet of paper. Check transparencies for misspellings and grammatical errors. Spelling and grammar checkers on word processing software make this an easy task. If you expect your students to spell correctly in their assignments, you need to model good spelling yourself.

(5) Write only key words, phrases, diagrams, and formulas.

There is something attractive about writing on the overhead transparencies. New teachers who use the blackboard effectively suddenly start writing copiously when using the overhead projector. They start taking notes for students on the overhead. Taking notes for the students keeps a teacher overly busy. It is hard to monitor student understanding if you are occupied writing. You can prompt students to take notes by including a few key words on the overhead projector, but do not take notes for them.

(6) Read the text aloud for auditory learners.

Auditory learners, those students who learn best by listening, appreciate you reading what is written on the transparency. Do not expect your class to read and instantly understand the image on the screen.

Sometimes I feel rather silly reading the words on the screen. I think I should be enlarging on the major points with amusing illustrations and witty one-liners; however, I remind myself that I must make the major points before I embellish them.

(7) Use colors to emphasize important concepts or facts.

Advertisers use color to gain and keep people's attention; color works for teachers too. For example, a black line of text with one key word in red is memorable. Also, remember to use high-contrasting colors—not yellow on a white background—for legibility. The occasional use of color for emphasis is memorable, but using a rainbow of colors in one line of text makes it difficult to read. Color printers are readily accessible and create wonderful transparencies. If you do not have access to a color printer, you can use colored highlighters; however, when choosing colors remember that some students are red-green colorblind.

(8) Make transparencies legible.

This should go without saying; however, I have had to struggle in the back of many classrooms trying to read images on a screen. I recall especially struggling to read the numbers and units on graphs and key words on diagrams. Even textbook publishers make lettering too small on transparencies. For example, one biology intern was the proud owner of a set of color transparencies acquired from a trade show. He used one of his transparencies in a lesson I observed and evaluated. We both were dismayed that we could not see the key words on the diagrams from the back row. He mentioned the problem to his class. In response, one of the students suggested laying a clear transparency over the colored transparency and writing in big print the key words he wanted to explain. The solution was simple and low tech. It also allowed the teacher to highlight only the relevant information on the prepared transparency.

I suggest that you place only three to five points on a transparency. More than five will require such small lettering that students in the back of the classroom will not be able to read the image on the screen. I make most of my overheads with twenty-four–point (one-third inch) Helvetica Bold lettering. It is sufficiently large and dark to be seen in the back of an average-sized classroom.

These eight tips may seem simple, but I frequently see teachers, speakers, and other presenters making the errors that prompted these guidelines. Perhaps by my calling common errors to your attention, you can avoid making the same mistakes.

PowerPoint Use

More and more secondary classrooms are equipped with computers with cables connected to data projectors or televisions. This makes the use of PowerPoint presentations possible. PowerPoint and other presentation software have made it easy for teachers to capture pictures and videos from the World Wide Web and other sources and bring beautiful and memorable images into the classroom. To capture the attention of the current generation of "digital natives" in secondary school, we as teachers need to use Web-based and instructional computing technologies.

As an earth science teacher, I frequently visited the NASA Web site to copy dramatic satellite images taken of planets, galaxies, and nebulae. I also used the United State Geologic Survey Web site to find volcanoes in full eruption. My students loved the large images that provided more detail than their textbooks. Their eyes were glued to the screen when I showed pyroclastic flows and lava pouring out of vents in the Earth.

Currently, student teachers like to insert YouTube videos into their PowerPoint presentations. A few minutes of action, narration, and music can enliven a lecture. Of course the quality of videos on YouTube varies greatly. I have found excellent documentaries by BBC as well as some poorly focused videos by other sources. Because of such varying quality and unknown content, make sure that you preview all videos before you show them to a class.

The most common error I see today in PowerPoint presentations is that the teacher puts too many ideas on one slide. The rule of thumb is three to five bulleted points per slide. If you have more than five bullets, the chances are that you have to use such a small font that the people in the back of the room cannot read your words. Also, you are probably giving out too much information. Please recall that people remember small clusters better than long strings of information.

Each slide should take a minute or less to talk through. You can explain three bullet points in a minute. If you need to elaborate a point, give it a separate slide with its own bullet points and illustrations. By using this general rule, you can also gauge the length in minutes of your lecture.

With all of the backgrounds available for PowerPoint presentations, use caution in selecting one. Does the background detract from the presentation?

I know bright and multicolored backgrounds are festive, but they may detract from student attention to content and illustrations. Light-colored backgrounds are best. I recommend using the same background consistently throughout a presentation.

Transitions between slides are important. Most often they should be inconspicuous (for example, one slide is instantly replaced by the next, or one slide dissolves quickly into the next) to not distract the learner. However, once in a while a key word swooping in can be memorable. Nevertheless, too many dramatic transitions can be counterproductive. I once watched a dignified professor present a PowerPoint on curricular analysis that a graduate student made. Each new title came swooping in from the left and over the top. It was distracting at best. However, it was a nightmare when someone requested that the professor back up five slides to review a point. The audience had to wait while the text repeatedly swooped in. The audience grew impatient and the professor annoyed.

In the event that your PowerPoint does not go as planned and you have to exit the presentation to fix it, please remember that although you are busy and riveted by taking care of the problem, your audience is disengaged. The same is true of surfing on the Internet. Surfing is engrossing to the one who is doing it; however, for the spectator, it can be boring. To avoid downtime for surfing, you can insert hyperlinks into your PowerPoint presentations so that Web sites automatically open when you click on the hyperlink from presentation mode. This creates a smooth transition from one form of multimedia to another without having to minimize one and open another.

Some tips for whiteboard and transparency use also apply to PowerPoint presentations:

- Display only key words, phrases, diagrams, and formulas for your students.
- Reinforce the image on the screen by reading the text for auditory learners.
- Use color occasionally to emphasize important concepts, facts, and so forth.
- Make slides legible (that is, use a font size big enough to read in the back of the room).

PowerPoint presentations also provide some unique challenges. The most obvious is to make transitions between slides inconspicuous, so not to distract the learner. An occasional title swooping onto the screen can be entertaining, but too often such transitions are time-consuming and distract from the content.

Summary

The most notable errors in presentation technique often involve the use of whiteboards, chalkboards, slides or images from overhead transparencies, and PowerPoint presentations. Here are five guidelines for whiteboard use:

- Speak, then write on the board;
- Speak while facing the class;
- Write key words, simple illustrations, and formulas;
- Place words and concepts according to importance; and
- Erase the board.

When using the overhead projector, remember that when you turn out the lights, the students tend to go to sleep. Here are eight tips for use of the overhead projector:

- Point to the image on the screen, not the transparency on the projector;
- Teach the students, not the projector;
- Move around the classroom;
- Prepare transparencies in advance;
- Write only key words, phrases, diagrams, and formulas for your students;
- Reinforce the image on the screen by reading the text for auditory learners;
- Use colors occasionally to emphasize important concepts, facts, and so forth; and
- Make the transparencies legible.

The last four tips are also applicable to PowerPoint presentations. Following these simple guidelines and tips will make your presentations more effective.

ONLINE RESOURCES

International Association of Science and Technology for Development. No date. Making PowerPoint Slides: Avoiding the Pitfalls of Bad Slides. http://www.iasted.org/conferences/formatting/presentations-tips.ppt (accessed July 14, 2010).

PowerPoint Presentation Advice. http://www.cob.sjsu.edu/splane_m/ PresentationTips.htm (accessed January 10, 2009).

Teach Republic. Know the write ways to use your whiteboard. http://articles. techrepublic.com.com/5100-10878_11-1030209.html (accessed January 10, 2009).

PART III

The Bigger Picture

Chapter 13

Boring Teachers

No teacher admits to being boring; yet, boring teachers abound. In fact, the proportion of boring teachers seems to increase with grade level. I do not know any boring kindergarten teacher—grumpy yes, boring no. Kindergarten teachers use a variety of methods and strategies to teach children through their five senses. Universities at the other end of formal education, however, are home to myriad boring teachers. At the university level, we often rely on assaulting only the sense of hearing using a barrage of concepts, ideas, and examples mixed together into a lecture. So where do all these boring professors and teachers go wrong? Let us examine some possibilities (See sidebar 13.1.)

New teachers tend to teach in two general patterns. They either imitate the way they were taught, or they teach as they learn best (Ebeling 2000). I see student teachers presenting lessons in the same way they were taught the lesson four to forty years ago. For example, they drill students on spelling lists orally. This way of teaching spelling is probably a relic of the near-paperless classrooms and spelling bees of previous centuries. Today, we rarely spell anything aloud; we write by hand or type into a computer. It makes sense to teach children spelling in a manner that reflects the way they will use the skill in life. Sometimes, tradition has an inappropriately strong influence in today's classrooms. The second pattern new teachers fall into is teaching in the way they learn best. For example, some students learn well by reading a chapter and then answering the questions at the end of the chapter to check their comprehension; others learn most effectively by reading the questions at the end of the chapter and then digging through the chapter to find answers. In the end, both types of students learn the material equally well. However, a new teacher may insist that students read the chapter and then answer the questions because that is how the teacher learns best. (In chapter 14, "Not Everyone Learns the Same Way You Do," I discuss learning styles and describe some of the many ways people learn. You will learn how to teach to engage many types of learners.)

These two patterns of teaching—teaching how you were taught and teaching how you learn best—do not form an adequate teaching repertoire. Good teachers apply a complex set of skills. Good teaching, by the way, is based on the application of the results of rigorous behavior, learning, and brain research. I do not expect you to learn about this research during this initial period in your teacher-education program, but be assured that good educational practices are more than someone's opinion.

Child and Adult Perspectives on Teaching

The practice of teaching is quite different from the perception of teaching that we had as children and adolescents. Adolescents may envy the power teachers have over students and classroom activities, but teachers facing a classroom of students for the first time—with thirty pairs of expectant eyes on them—feel anxiety, not power. As you step into the role of an instructor, reflect on how your perception of teaching has changed since you were a child. Do not forget your childhood perceptions from the other side of the desk; they will help you gain insight.

Teaching in the New Millennium

The image of teachers pouring information into a student's head is outdated. Today we think of students as active, not passive, learners. Students are encouraged to create their own knowledge through active involvement in the learning process (for example, constructivism). This process is highly personal. Each individual has a unique combination of strengths, weaknesses, and preferences in learning. Also, each student filters new information through her/his life experiences. In today's classroom, good teachers try to celebrate and honor diversity. In years past, students were supposed to learn in whatever way the teacher dictated. Today, we tend to give students choices on how they want to learn. We teach through a variety of methods so students have the opportunity to excel using their academic strengths and to grow by developing their weaker skills. Today, students are educational consumers; gone are the days when they would sit through whatever class their guidance counselor, parent, or advisor recommended. Now, students actively seek good learning situations for themselves and complain if they do not get what they want or need. Although passive students still exist, the proportion is decreasing.

As students take a more active approach to learning, the teacher's role is also changing. Teachers must be able to use a variety of instructional methods (for example, interactive lecture, discussion, hands-on activities, simulations, and group work) and assessment techniques (for example, essay exams, group projects, laboratory practical exams, portfolios) in addition to the traditional multiple-choice examination. The teacher must be a facilitator and coach as well as a traditional instructor.

Student bodies in the new millennium are far more diverse, especially in urban settings. Students from dozens of different ethnic groups can attend the same secondary school. Teachers are faced with engaging all students while taking into account differences in their cultural heritage, class, and language.

As in previous decades, good teaching looks effortless. In reality, it is the result of extensive planning, good preparation, study, observation of good teaching practices, experimentation, reflection, and self-analysis.

Self-Improvement

You are probably reading this book because you want to be a better teacher. Desire is the primary ingredient for improvement; observation, self-analysis, and experimentation will also help you improve. You can develop these skills.

The first step necessary is to be reflective. When I teach swimming classes, I tell my students that thinking swimmers improve faster than swimmers who do not think about their technique. I encourage them to concentrate on their stroke technique rather than simply trying to reach the other side of the pool. I make the same request of my students entering the teaching profession. I ask them to be analytical and reflective teachers. To start, ask yourself, "How can I improve this lesson?" and "Did my students respond well to what I did?"

Another skill to develop is your power of observation. When I attend a presentation, I analyze the presenter's clarity and teaching techniques. This habit is a consequence of one of the duties of my profession, helping novice teachers improve their classroom performance. I typically watch students perform skills described in this book. I suggest you watch good teachers as they use these skills. Ask yourself: How do they implement a skill? Could I use that technique in my classroom? Do not expect to implement every variation of skills and techniques in your classroom; not every technique will work for you. Conversely, not everything you do will work for other teachers. Also, learn to observe your students' learning. Students give many subtle clues about your teaching and their learning processes. For example, listen to their points of confusion. If you detect the same confusion more than once, you probably need to modify your lesson to make it clearer; also, more thoroughly explain parts that are potentially confusing and move through the material more slowly.

Developing self-analysis and observation skills will help you to improve over the course of your teaching career. See sidebar 13.2 for characteristics of a boring teacher.

The High Cost of Boring Teachers and Schools

Unfortunately, the dropout rate for high school students in the United States is about 30 percent, and even higher for some minorities. Students cite the main reason that they drop out of school is that classes are not interesting (Bridgeland, Dilulio, and Morrison 2006). That must mean there is a lot of uninteresting curriculum being mandated by states and provinces. A teacher, however, can make curriculum more interesting. If we unpack the adolescent complaint of "not interesting," I suspect the students mean not relevant to their lives or the lives they would like to lead. By weaving in examples from the daily life of adolescents, a teacher can make high school more interesting. Also in the bigger picture, such a teacher is providing a quality education that will retain students in school.

Keeping adolescents in school is important. Studies show that high school graduates are more successful in society (for example, get jobs with benefits, stay out of prison, and do not require social assistance such as food stamps) and also command higher paychecks than dropouts. Higher paychecks contribute to greater economic stability for individuals and often families.

If we connect the dots, we see that teachers who strive to keep their classes interesting contribute greatly to society and community well-being. (Bravo!)

Summary

Teaching in the new century is different than in previous decades. Presenting lessons in the same way you were taught or the way that you learn best may not be effective or pertinent for present-day society. Today students are encouraged to construct their own knowledge through active involvement in the learning process. Teachers are using a variety of instructional methods and evaluations, becoming facilitators of learning as well as traditional teachers.

Observation, reflection, self-analysis, and experimentation will help you become a more effective and higher-quality teacher.

REFERENCES

Ebeling, D. G. 2000. Adapting Your Teaching to Any Learning Style. *Phi Delta Kappan* 82: 247–48.

ONLINE RESOURCES

Bridgeland, J. M., J. J. Dilulio, and K. B. Morison. 2006. *The Silent Epidemic: Perspective of High School Dropouts.* The Gates Foundation. http://www.gatesfoundation.org/united-states/Documents/TheSilentEpidemic-ExecSum.pdf (accessed March 1, 2006).

Constructivism (learning theory). http://en.wikipedia.org/wiki/Constructivism_ (learning_theory) (accessed January 10, 2009).

Instructional strategies—History, Nature and Categories of Instructional Strategies, Instructional strategies and learner outcomes http://education. stateuniversity.com/pages/2099/Instructional-Strategies.html (accessed January 10, 2009).

Chapter 14

Not Everyone Learns the Same Way You Do

New teachers tend to imitate the way they were taught or they teach the way they learn best (Ebeling 2000). Both of these bring some measure of success to the classroom; yet, many students struggle to learn. Many of them feel like unsuccessful learners, because the way they have been taught does not match the way they learn best.

Until the mid-1970s, educational research focused on finding the best method for teaching everyone. Now we are aware that there is not one best method of teaching and learning for everyone. Educators now recognize that not everyone learns the same way and each student has his or her own preferred ways of learning (ASCD n.d.; Dunn and Griegs 1995; Ebeling 2000; Guild and Garger 1985; Kolb 1983; Leaver 1997; McCarthy 1987; Samples 1994). These preferred ways of learning are called *learning styles*. Although each person's learning style is unique, these styles fall into major groups. In this chapter, I primarily discuss the most common learning styles.

Variety—the Spice of Life and Learning

When I teach a unit on learning styles to pre-service teachers, I begin by placing large pieces of newsprint around the room with fill-in-the-blank statements about how students like to learn and study. For example, I can concentrate best at ____ o'clock. If I have to study for a tough final, I like to _____. I can study ____ minutes before I need a break. I learn best from _____ (for example, lectures, reading, discussion, doing something with my hands, planning and doing a project). The students write their answers and we analyze them. We never fail to have a variety of answers. Students like to study at all times of day and night. Some like to work alone and others in a group. Some can study only for short periods and others in marathon sessions. Some do one project at a time and others do several. Some get overloaded with large quantities of information given in a short period, and others are stimulated by it. Some learn from lecture, others discussion, others from listening and talking to friends, and others through doing projects. It appears there are many roads to academic success. One uncomfortable conclusion that arises from the analysis of the student responses is that the existing diversity of learning preferences is not matched by the diversity of teaching styles and learning opportunities in an average school setting.

Theories abound on how to be academically successful. My father said, "Study in the morning, when your mind is fresh." He also advised me that I did not need to cram for a test if I studied all semester and listened carefully in lecture. My mom instructed me to turn off the radio while studying. Other parents were sure that sitting at a table with a good light aided studying. My parents were mostly right for me. I study well in the morning and in a quiet setting. I learn well from lectures. I found, however, that even if I had studied all semester, I still needed to cram for a final exam. I also read well curled up in a comfortable chair with a warm comforter. I have friends, however, who cannot find a book, let alone their place in it, before noon, who do not listen to lecture but excel in the laboratory, who fall asleep while reading in a warm place, and who only study before a final. Because their study habits match their learning styles, my friends do well in school.

Adults tend to understand their own learning preferences. We automatically seek out learning situations that are good for us. For example, I heard one friend say, "I've got to get away for a minute to read this." She meant she had to escape the noise of her home and find a quiet spot to read and comprehend information. Children and adolescents, however, do not understand their own learning preferences as well as adults do. I have seen a young child sitting in the living room reading and rereading a chapter in a book. She did not realize the noise around her interfered with her reading comprehension. As educators, it is important that we understand enough about learning styles to provide a learning environment in which all students can thrive, and it is important to create a variety of activities that our students can learn from.

Modalities

One of the ways to categorize learning styles is by modality. "A *modality* is a sensory channel through which a person receives and retains information. The modalities which are the most important to educators are auditory, visual, and kinesthetic-tactile (Guild and Garger 1985)" (McKeown 2003, 872). Furthermore, "Auditory learners use their voices and ears as primary modes of learning. Auditory learners remember what they hear and what they express verbally. When they have difficulty learning, they tend to talk things through.

As learners, they thrive in discussions, appreciate the teacher's explanations, and remember assignments that are given orally" (McKeown 2003, 872).

During my third year of university teaching, I was puzzled by one of my students. She was an attentive student but rarely took notes in my class; she excelled on the assignments and tests. Usually, students who do not take notes do not do well in my class. I asked her how she learned. She explained that she learned by listening. She took a few notes, but they were not the mainstay of her learning, nor was reading. She was a classic auditory learner. Her A+ average attested to the fact that auditory learners can excel in traditional classrooms and university settings.

Visual learners "remember what they see—written works, pictures, graphs, maps, movies, and art, for example." "Visual learners picture in their minds what is being described." They understand and remember illustrations, charts, diagrams, outlines, and maps. "They appreciate pleasant physical surroundings" and the teacher using illustrations (for example, overhead transparencies and slides). They remember assignments that are written down (McKeown 2003, 872).

One of my students was an extremely visual learner. I asked him how he survived in a university setting, where much of the information is given in lecture format. He replied that he took notes in class and then wrote them in outline form. Then, he copied the outline until he understood the structure of the information and had memorized it. He, too, was an A student.

"Kinesthetic-tactile learners like to touch things and be physically involved in what they study. As learners, they like to be busy—making a product, acting out a situation, or doing a project. They thrive in laboratory settings where they can experiment, practice, and try new things. All this activity helps them to understand and to remember" (McKeown 2003, 872).

Another one of my students seemed to doze through lecture and mumble through discussions, but in a laboratory setting he came alive. He smiled and joked as he put apparatus together; he fearlessly moved through experiments. Afterward, he explained the experiment and principles behind it. He was a kinesthetic-tactile learner; he also had good grades.

"Successful learners often function in more than one modality. Multi-modality students have a higher chance of success because they have a broad range of situations through which they can learn. Students with one modal strength can become stronger students by transferring information from a weaker mode to a stronger one" (McKeown 2003, 872). For example, the visual learner described above transferred what he learned by listening in lecture into a written outline. The outline gave him visual clues to help him understand and remember.

So, how do you teach students of all three modalities? Plan your lessons so that all students hear, see, and do each time you present a new set of concepts. Be systematic about engaging students of each modality. If a student does not understand an idea you present in one modality, present it again in another modality. For example, if a student cannot remember a vocabulary word you give orally, write it on the board, or let him/her write it in a notebook.

You can help students develop their weaker modalities by helping them practice types of learning that are not naturally easy for them. Most children and about one-third of high school students are kinesthetic-tactile learners. It is important to their success that we do not teach them through talking, which is the current norm.

Perception and Processing

David Kolb framed another method to categorize learning styles. In his system, learning is divided into two parts. The first is perception—how we take in information. The second is processing—what we do with that information. The combination of perception and processing forms our learning style.

Perception is characterized as a continuum from abstract conceptualization to concrete experience. *Abstract learners* step outside the experience and analyze it. *Concrete learners* prefer to step inside an experience and use their five senses to perceive. For example, a concrete learner and an abstract learner go to a party. The abstract learner stands by the door surveying the situation and decides she does not want to stay. The concrete learner joins the party, talks to a few people, tastes the hors d' oeuvres, and decides she does not want to stay at the party. Both types of learners have an equally valuable way of perceiving the situation.

Processing is characterized as a continuum from reflective observation to active experimentation. To illustrate the two ends of the continuum, let me describe how two different students approach learning a new computer application. Both students are told they must learn to use a new computer program that creates flowcharts. The *active learner* would sit down in front of the computer and start moving the mouse, clicking on menus and buttons and typing in commands until s/he masters the program. In contrast, the *reflective learner* would watch someone successfully use the program and consult the manual before sitting down to use the program. Both the active experimenter and the reflective observer are successful and learn the program equally well. Both ways of learning should be equally valued by their instructor and society.

Kolb crosses the processing and perceiving continuums, which results in four learning styles: divergers, assimilators, convergers, and accommodators.

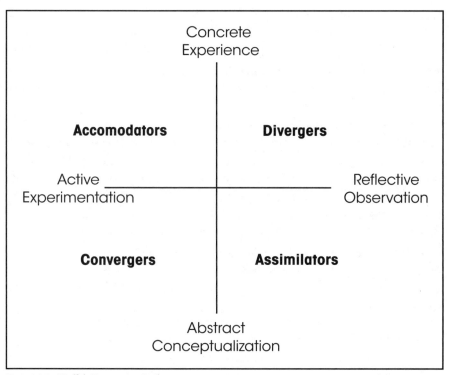

Concrete
Experience

Accomodators   **Divergers**

Active _____ _____ Reflective
Experimentation   Observation

Convergers   **Assimilators**

Abstract
Conceptualization

Fig. 14.1. Kolb's Learning Styles.

Each group has its own distinctive strengths as learners and each has an equally valid way of learning. The four learning styles are distributed nearly evenly throughout the general population.

Divergers perceive information concretely and process it reflectively. They seek personal meaning. They often learn by listening and sharing their ideas. These students often excel in discussion and are motivated to learn when they see a personal connection between their lives and the topic.

Assimilators perceive information abstractly and process it reflectively. They seek knowledge that leads to conceptual understanding. They learn well in a traditional classroom listening to experts and thinking things through. These students often find new ideas fascinating, and they value data. Assimilators traditionally have been thought of as model students; they learn well from lecture.

Convergers perceive information abstractly and process it actively. They seek understanding of how things work. They are good at integrating theory and practice and applying common sense. They learn well through laboratory activities and problem-solving exercises. These students thrive in laboratory-based science curriculum and activity-based classes where they learn from doing.

Accommodators perceive information concretely and process it actively. They seek self-discovery. They integrate experience and application. They are often excited about new things; they like change and are flexible. They learn well through doing projects.

People of each one of these learning styles have remarkable talents and contribute in differing and valuable ways to our society. If you look at a major construction project, you will see how each type of learner contributes to the project's success. For example, let us look at building a boat. Divergers will talk to people who will use the boat to identify and articulate the boat users' various needs. Using this information, the assimilators will create a plan for the boat that is based on sound theories and principles. Convergers, then, will build the boat from the plans, and accommodators will navigate the boat to its planned destination and many places beyond. The successful completion and use of the boat was made possible only by tapping the various talents of people of all four learning styles.

Teachers need to step into different roles to teach each type of these learners. For divergers, the teacher is a motivator who creates a reason for the student to learn. For example, the teacher creates a list of discussion questions, which personalizes a concept for the students. For assimilators, the teacher steps into the traditional teaching role to give students—often through lecture—the facts, principles, and generalizations that lead them to greater understanding. For convergers, the teacher acts as a coach or facilitator, letting the students try out or experiment with ideas, concepts, processes, and so forth. For example, the teacher may create a laboratory activity that demonstrates a principle presented in a reading assignment. For accommodators, the teacher is an evaluator or remediator, letting the students teach themselves and others. For example, the teacher assigns a project at the end of a unit. While the students are creating their projects, the teacher acts as a tutor, a resource person, or a critiquing audience (Kolb 1983; McCarthy 1987).

Multiple Intelligences

Howard Gardner, with his work on multiple intelligences, presents another way to think about the variety of talents and skills that the students in your classroom possess. This work revolutionized how the world thinks of intelligence. Prior to Gardner's work, the public and educational community measured and interpreted intelligence using standardized tests and intelligence quotient

(IQ) scores. Intelligence was summarized in a two- or three-digit number derived from taking a pencil and paper test. This number was thought to be fixed at birth and largely reflected linguistic and logical-mathematical reasoning. In *Frames of Mind,* Gardner defined intelligence as solving a problem or creating a product that is valued in a culture. This definition expanded the concept of intelligence to include such culturally valued abilities as navigation, sculpture, and dance. Gardner (1983) proposed the existence of seven separate human intelligences. They are:

- "Linguistic intelligence involves sensitivity to spoken and written language, the ability to learn languages, and the capacity to use language to accomplish certain goals. Lawyers, speakers, writers, poets are among the people with high linguistic intelligence" (Gardner 1999, 41).
- "Logical-mathematical intelligence involves the capacity to analyze problems logically, carry out mathematical operations, and investigate issues scientifically. Mathematicians, logicians, and scientists exploit logical-mathematical intelligence" (Gardener 1999, 42).
- "Musical intelligence entails skill in the performance, composition, and appreciation of musical patterns" (Gardner 1999, 42).
- "Bodily-kinesthetic intelligence entails the potential of using one's whole body or parts of the body (like the hand or the mouth) to solve problems or fashion products" (Gardner 1999, 41). "Dancers, actors, and athletes" use this intelligence, as do "crafts persons, surgeons, bench-top scientists, mechanics, and many other technically oriented professionals" (Gardner 1999, 41).
- "Spatial intelligence features the potential to recognize and manipulate the patterns of wide space . . . as well as the patterns of more confined areas" (Gardener 1999, 42). Pilots and navigators use wide space, while chess players, artists, and architects use confined space.
- "Interpersonal intelligence denotes a person's capacity to understand the intentions, motivations, and desires of other people and, consequently, to work effectively with others. Salespeople, teachers, clinicians, religious leaders, political leaders, and actors all need acute interpersonal intelligence" (Gardner 1999, 43).
- "Intrapersonal intelligence involves the capacity to understand oneself, to have an effective working model of oneself—including one's own desires, fears, and capacities—and to use such information effectively in regulating one's own life" (Gardner 1999, 43).

Equity in the Classroom

From this short description of learning modalities, learning styles, and multiple intelligences, you can see that people learn in different ways. In response, educators have the responsibility of using a variety of teaching methods to reach all of our students. It is not important that you know the learning style of each one of your students; it is important, however, that you teach to engage learners of all styles. This attention to a balanced variety of instructional techniques is equity in action.

All students should be given an equal chance to learn, regardless of their learning style. All students should be given the opportunity to do their best work, to learn in the mode that is most comfortable for them, and to feel successful as a learner. To accomplish this, we teachers need to give a variety of assignments that use the talents associated with each learning style. That way, every student will have a chance to shine.

Conversely, each student should also be given the opportunity to stretch and grow, to learn how to learn in ways that are not as comfortable or easy, and to gain new skills and confidence in themselves as learners. To accomplish this, we need to make sure that we give assignments that help students develop skills that do not come naturally to them.

Fortunately, most classes have a mix of students of all four learning styles. Every assignment allows some students to shine by exercising their strongest skills, while helping others to grow by developing their weaker skills. Students who find the assignment easy can help students who are having difficulty. This student-led teaching helps reinforce students' new knowledge and confidence in their abilities.

Evaluation (that is, grading) should also honor and involve students of all learning styles. If you only grade students on one type of activity (for example, multiple-choice tests) you are not testing in all learning styles. Everyone should have the opportunity of being evaluated on their best work some of the time. If we use a variety of assessment techniques, students will also be evaluated in ways that are more challenging to them. In my courses, I evaluate participation in discussions, comprehension of lectures and readings, performance in laboratory activities, and the products of projects. In this way, the final grade reflects student performance in assignments that call on the strengths of all four learning styles.

To bring the evaluation issue home, I do the following activity with prospective teachers. I ask them to grasp their pencils with their nonwriting hands. Then, I ask them to sign their name. Next, I walk around the room, grading each signature. Most students receive a D or an F. Then, I lead a discussion about how it feels to be graded on work that is less than their best. Students respond that they are angry and upset; the grading was unfair. Then, we talk about fairness and grading students in their areas of strengths and areas of weakness. Finally, I ask the students to sign their name ten times with their nonwriting hand. Most students see a remarkable improvement in this short practice session. I close the class by asking, "Now that you have had a chance to practice developing a difficult skill and improve, how would you feel about being graded on your work?" The majority feel much better about it. I use this activity to explore equity in grading in relation to learning styles.

By systematically teaching to engage students of all learning styles, teachers engage all of their students. Many teachers hope that everyone enjoys their class at some point and is challenged at others. Everyone should have the satisfaction and pleasure of enjoying learning.

Learning-Style Philosophy

Underlying the use of learning styles is the philosophy that all students are valuable and should be equally valued by the education community. Unfortunately, that is not the case in our schools. Students who learn well in the passive mode—listening, reflecting, and abstract conceptualization—have been rewarded. Students who learn well in the active mode—doing, talking, active experimentation, and concrete experiences—have often had their learning needs ignored. In a way, this is a form of discrimination and inequity that we hope to extinguish as our society moves toward greater equity.

This world would be a much less enjoyable place if we had only learners of one or two styles. The diversity of learners gives us strength and depth to accomplish complex tasks. For fun, let us look at the crew of the starship *Enterprise* of the television series *Star Trek: The Next Generation* to see how the characters' learning styles contribute to their success. The main crew forms a team; each member of that team has different strengths. Deanna Troi, the ship's counselor, is a diverger talented in her gestalt understanding of her own and others' personal meaning and motivation. Data is an assimilator who values information, theories, and equations and has tremendous conceptual understanding. Geordi, the engineer, is a converger who can apply abstract theory in the engine room. Captain Jean-Luc Picard is an accommodator who excels at pulling ideas from each of his crew and synthesizing them into a plan of action, which he then implements. The learning styles and diverse talents of these characters contribute to the repeated success of the space exploration program.

Your classroom may not be as exciting as an episode of *Star Trek,* but your students are probably as diverse as the crew of the *Enterprise.*

The learning-styles philosophy also carries with it a celebration of diversity. Celebration is difficult, especially when some students drive you crazy. I have one good friend and colleague who admitted that each year in her classes, there would be one child who got on her nerves. It occurred to her after learning-styles training that the child invariably would have the opposite learning style from hers. Her comments made me reflect on students who had tried my patience. I would complain, "I wish they were more organized." "I wish they would read their books." "I wish they would speak up when they do not understand." "I wish, I wish, I wish. . . ." It occurred to me that I was wishing the students were more like me. That was a rude awakening. I thought I was celebrating diversity in my classroom, but my wishes were toward uniformity. Then I thought, "Good grief, teaching a classroom full of people just like me would be a nightmare come true." Since that time, I have tried to be more insightful and complimentary of the diverse talents of my students and more sympathetic toward their weaknesses.

The learning-styles philosophy also calls for honesty in self-evaluation. Are you spending equal time and effort to engage students of all learning styles? It is easy to think you have taught all students equally if you had five minutes of discussion, twenty-five minutes of lecture with three illustrations, and fifteen minutes of hands-on activity each day, complemented by one project every three weeks. Technically, you would have used a variety of methods that called on the strengths of different learning styles; however, you would not have given equal time to each.

The consequences of not engaging students of all learning styles are unfortunate. Dunn and Griggs (1995) state, "findings suggest that students whose instruction is not responsive to their learning styles achieve significantly less well than children whose instruction is responsive to their learning styles" (3). Leaver (1997) describes the ways that students of specific learning modalities are left wanting by teachers who predominantly teach through their own learning styles. Leaver states, "Students with learning styles that differ from those of their teachers lose daily battles in the style wars" (69). For example, auditory students often fail to get the aural support they need from visual teachers who primarily enrich their classes with handouts, overhead transparencies, and videos. Leaver continues, "Kinesthetic learners in classes taught by visual and auditory teachers are often immobilized. . . . They are so often told to sit still and pay attention" (71). Some of the symptoms of mismatched learning and teaching styles are completing the wrong homework, suddenly doing poorly in a favorite subject area, disinterest, and low motivation (Leaver 1995).

Awareness and Responsibility

In this chapter, I have tried to raise your awareness of learning styles and how you can respond to your students' different needs. You can provide a variety of learning opportunities by using diverse activities, assignments, and methods of evaluation. As educators, it is our responsibility to be equitable and embrace diversity; we can use our knowledge of learning styles to promote equity and diversity in the classroom.

To discover your own learning style, you may want to find and take a learning style or modality inventory on the Internet. It may help you understand your own educational history and uncover some of your teaching biases.

Summary

New teachers teach in two general patterns: (1) they imitate the way they were taught, or (2) they teach the way they learn best. Alone, these two methods fall short of meeting the needs of all learners.

Modalities are the sensory channels through which a person receives and retains information. Three modalities are important to educators:

- auditory,
- visual, and
- kinesthetic-tactile.

Another commonly used way to categorize learning styles is through the way people

- perceive information—abstract conceptualization to concrete experience, and
- process information—reflective observation to active experimentation.

Another way to think about the diverse abilities students bring to your classroom is through Howard Gardner's multiple intelligences: linguistic, logical mathematical, musical, bodily-kinesthetic, spatial, interpersonal, and intrapersonal.

Many home-spun ideas and misconceptions surround how to be academically successful. In truth, many ways of learning lead to academic success. Students of all learning styles should be valued in your classroom and given an equal chance to learn.

REFERENCES

Association for Supervision and Curriculum Development. No date. *Learning a Matter of Style,* Part I [Videotape]. Alexandria, Va.: Association for Supervision and Curriculum Development.

Dunn, R., and S. A. Griggs. 1988. *Learning Styles: Quiet revolution in American secondary schools.* Reston, Va.: National Association of Secondary School Principals. Virgina: Association for Supervision and Curriculum Development.

Ebeling, D. G. 2000. Adapting your teaching to any learning style. *Phi Delta Kappan* 82: 247–48.

Gardner, H. 1983. *Frames of Mind: The theory of multiple intelligences.* New York: Basic Books.

Gardner, H. 1999. *Intelligence Reframed: Multiple intelligences for the 21st century.* New York: Basic Books.

Guild, P. B., and S. Garger. 1985. *Marching to Different Drummers.* Alexandria, Va.: Association for Supervision and Curriculum Development.

Kolb, D. A. 1983. *Experiential Learning: Experience as the source of learning and development.* Englewood Cliffs, N.J.: Prentice Hall.

Leaver, B. L. 1997. *Teaching the Whole Class.* Fourth edition. Thousand Oaks, Calif.: Corwin Press.

McCarthy, B. 1987. *The 4MAT System: Teaching to learning styles with right/left mode techniques.* Barrington, Ill.: Excel.

McKeown, R. 2003. Working with K–12 schools: Insights for scientists. *BioScience* 53: 870–75.

Samples, B. 1994. Instructional diversity. *The Science Teacher* 61(2): 14–17.

ONLINE RESOURCES

Wikipedia. Learning Styles. http://en.wikipedia.org/wiki/Learning_styles (accessed January 11, 2009).

LdPride.net. Learning Styles Explained. http://www.ldpride.net/learningstyles.MI.htm (accessed January 11, 2009).

Learning Styles. Learning Styles Community. http://www.learningstyles.net/ (accessed January 11, 2009).

Chapter 15

Be Kind

When I ask pre-service teachers about their favorite K-12 teachers, they often respond that the teachers were kind, fair, enthusiastic, loved teaching their disciplines, or helped students learn. Descriptions such as unkind, arbitrary, angry, and unfair do not enter the discussion. I have found that kindness can produce goodwill, cooperation, and effort in the classroom.

Does expressing kindness mean that you are a softy or you have to lower your expectations or standards for work? NO! Kindness expresses itself in the classroom through respect, common courtesy, and support for your students' efforts to learn.

Respect

Showing respect for your students' presence, ideas, and efforts is a powerful classroom tool. The Golden Rule—do unto others as you would have them do unto you—is appropriate. As long as teachers hold a position of power, there will be some who will abuse it. All of us have had teachers who were grumpy, seemed arbitrary, and wielded their power to give us a rotten grade or send us to the principal. Thank goodness, they were the exception, not the rule. Although teachers assume authority over their classrooms, they should exercise that authority with benevolence and respect.

The most pleasant and best-run classrooms I have observed were based on respect. The teachers treated students with respect; in return, the students respected the teachers and one another. All this respectfulness was the result of solid discipline plans written and implemented by the teachers. Students were treated with respect, given guidelines for respectful behavior, and reminded to act respectfully toward one another during student reports. These classrooms were pleasant to visit and to learn in. By the way, these teachers did not have special, high-achieving, or mannerly students. They were peers of the students down the hall who gave their teachers a bad time and repeatedly made inappropriate comments to one another.

Common Courtesy

Teachers must treat students with the same courtesy they expect to receive. Just as doctors, lawyers, and bankers are courteous to their clients, effective teachers extend common courtesy to their students. Common courtesies include listening carefully when spoken to, saying excuse me when passing through crowded spaces, saying thank you, being reasonably pleasant to be around, being sensitive to body language, respecting students' personal space and property, and not intentionally embarrassing students. Fortunately, reminding most teachers to treat their students with common courtesy is unnecessary. Courtesy in the classroom is another area for occasional self-evaluation.

Teachers constantly model behavior to their students. Students continually observe their teachers' actions and interactions with students. Adolescents emulate the behavior of people they want to be like. If you treat your students with respect and courtesy, you probably will have more courteous and respectful students.

Most people know the rules of common courtesy, but they choose to use them selectively. In my childhood, teachers commanded a great deal of respect and deferential treatment from students and parents. Perhaps, new teachers who grew up in similar circumstances think they should automatically receive respect and deferential treatment owing to their positions. If they are not granted this, they may respond gruffly. To prevent yourself from falling into the same trap, think about how you can earn the respect of your students and the community.

Support Your Students' Efforts to Learn

Supporting your students' efforts to learn will lead to productive learning. Support comes in both tangible and intangible forms. You can give tangible support by providing enough information or supplies when they are needed. Reference books, articles, and data to complete assignments or satisfy student curiosity are essential; scissors, paper, and glue may be necessary for other assignments. If you cannot provide classroom supplies because of budgetary reasons, warn your students in advance that they will need to bring them to class.

You can provide intangible support through verbal encouragement or praise for good effort or a job well done. A compliment can motivate students to continue achieving. In fact, small compliments can result in huge efforts on the students' part. I remember one compliment from a swimming buddy of mine. I was having a tough time at the beginning of a season. My stroke seemed ragged and my times were not improving. She said, "You are grabbing the water well; your hand is exiting the water where it went in." I was surprised; I had no idea my stroke was efficient. For the next several months, I worked hard and my times fell. The turning point arrived with one compliment.

One of my favorite memories of visiting high schools was an interchange between a student and her chemistry teacher. This master teacher allowed students to retake tests during a semester. His reasoning was that students had their own timetable for learning. As long as the students learned the material by the end of the grading period, he was satisfied. He said some students took six weeks to learn the material that had been presented in the first few weeks; then they understood enough to rapidly learn the remainder of the material. One girl in this category retook a test that she had failed the first time and received a good grade on it. She beamed and asked for study materials to retake the second test that she had done poorly on. As the teacher was getting the material, the student said, "If I get an A on the next retake and I get an A on the next test, I could get an A in the class." The teacher turned to her and said, "I would love to give you that A." A few weeks later, I saw the girl in class and asked her what grade she had received in chemistry. "An A!" she beamed. The teacher's support for her efforts paid off. The student was willing to work hard for a teacher who gave her the opportunity to succeed.

Setting Up Students for Success

Setting up your students for success is essential for good teaching. This action includes providing them with the resources, the information, the skills, and the environment necessary to satisfactorily complete an assignment. For example, a professor leading an aquatic ecology field trip for first-year students chooses a pond that is easy to sample and has abundant and diverse plant and animal life. He gives mini-lessons on the use of sampling equipment and supervises the more timid students' first attempts at using it. The students use the equipment to gather data. Upon analysis, the data reveals relationships typical of the results published in the textbook. The same professor chooses a pond that reveals atypical animal populations for his advanced students to survey. These students are challenged to find out by sampling for a variety of environmental indices why the populations are atypical. This professor has designed both field trips so that each group of students will have a successful learning experience.

Conversely, teachers also have the power to set up their students to fail. Teachers can assure failure by: not preparing students adequately for assignments; requesting that students always work in settings or modes that are opposite of their learning style; waiting to catch the students making mistakes;

giving examinations that are more difficult than the work assigned in class; belittling students' efforts; and undermining students' confidence as learners.

One thing you can do to set up students for success is to teach the skills they will need to be successful in your classroom. If your course is based on lecture, teach the students how to take notes. At the beginning of your course, you can leave time between major points for them to take notes; indicate what is important, and remind them to write it down. As the course progresses, you can lessen the time you wait between points and prompt them less frequently.

You might assume that older teenage learners, such as AP (Advanced Placement) and IB (International Baccalaureate) students, already know how to take notes, read textbooks, or have developed other learning skills. This is not a safe assumption. Some chagrined professors find that undergraduate freshmen flunking the midterm do not know how to read a textbook critically, or did not master basic study skills in high school. I know several full professors who risk the ill humor of their university students by teaching them basics at the beginning of a course. One physics professor advises his students to read the text with pencil and paper at hand. He encourages them to write out the mathematical formulas and work examples. His advice may seem overly simple, but students who heed his counsel generally find that they retain more of what they read. A little attention to students' needs at the beginning of a course can help them immeasurably later.

Attainable Assignments

Providing adequate support for your students is a form of kindness; making sure they have the skills or materials to accomplish assignments is essential. Ideal assignments are those that simultaneously help students stretch and grow while being attainable. Asking students to attempt assignments that you know they cannot complete is not only unkind but counterproductive to the learning process. Such assignments are not useful to teachers or students, especially if they result in a sense of failure.

Time to Adapt

In chapter 3, I discussed the importance of telling the class your rules at the beginning of the year or course. I also suggest that you give students time to adapt to your style of teaching and your grading procedures. For example, my ninth grade geography class entered high school accustomed to doing simple worksheets (for example, fill-in-the-blank and matching). When I gave them two-step map questions where information from one map must be compared with information on a second map to get an answer, some students dissolved in frustration. To help them, I modeled how to do a two-map comparison, and those who understood it tutored those who did not. Also, I let the students submit the assignment again and again until they got the score they wanted. I gave the students time to adjust to the reality that I was going to expect more of them than their previous social studies teachers.

Fatigue

Teaching is mentally, physically, and emotionally demanding. These demands result in fatigue. Fatigue strikes each teacher differently. Some teachers feel great all day, but collapse as soon as their students leave. Others slowly grow more tired throughout the day. Yet others have peaks and valleys of energy during the day. During demanding periods of the academic year, a deep fatigue can last from one day to the next. Regardless of the pattern, fatigue tends to shorten patience and raise tempers. At some time, all of us feel our patience wearing thin and our ability to respond with kindness dwindling.

When I feel my patience running out, I warn my students. Warnings are much better than explosions. At the beginning of one academic year, I told all of my Spanish classes that "a grinch lives in me." I also warned them that they never wanted to see the grinch and if they followed the class rules, they never would. Occasionally during the year, when their behavior was growing unacceptable, which I admit may have been because of my growing fatigue, I warned them, "You don't want to see the grinch."

Parting Comments

Midway through my second year of teaching, I came to realize how important a positive and consistent classroom environment was to my students. My sixth period class was a delight. They liked coming to class and I liked having them there. This was rare. My colleagues had warned me that the last period of the day was often the most difficult. By then the students were tired of being in school and teachers were frayed from hard work. As I looked at my grade book, I realized that many of the sixth period students were pulling Ds and Fs, especially the students with difficult home lives and learning disabilities. I marveled that in spite of their low grades, they wanted to come to my class, and they were learning at their own pace and level. If any of us messed up one day, the next was a new day and we could try again. After some reflection, it finally occurred to me that I had created a welcoming classroom where everyone knew the limits and felt safe. All those nights I had spent analyzing how I engaged students in learning and how I disciplined them were paying off.

This sixth period class also displayed their goodwill toward me when the principal came to my class to observe my teaching methods and abilities. That day, the students were attentive, engaged, well behaved, and good natured. The class went smoothly; the students stayed on task and demonstrated their knowledge. The principal was impressed, told me so, and wrote it into the formal evaluation. He also informally told me that we both knew the class did not always go that well. We both chuckled. The principal, however, did understand that I provided a positive classroom climate and created rapport with the students, which engendered such goodwill.

There is an adage that says, "You can catch more flies with honey than with vinegar." A little kindness and an underlying tone of respect from the teacher will improve the learning environment tremendously, while lending a feeling of security to the students. Students who are secure in the knowledge that teachers want them to succeed will strive and thrive in class.

Summary

Students and teachers tend to thrive in classrooms in which teachers

- Show respect for the students' presence, ideas, and efforts;
- Treat the students with common courtesy and kindness;
- Support student efforts to learn;
- Set up the students for success;
- Create attainable assignments; and
- Give students time to adapt to new instructional and grading methods.

ONLINE RESOURCES

Articlesbase.com. Creating Conducive Classroom Climate. http://www.articlesbase.com/education-articles/creating-conducive-classroom-climate-256406.html (accessed January 11, 2009).

WikEd. Classroom Climate. http://wik.ed.uiuc.edu/index.php/Classroom_Climate (accessed January 11, 2009).

PART IV

Becoming the Teacher You Want to Be

Chapter 16

Tensions of Practice Teaching

All student teachers, interns, and teacher candidates experience tensions during their school placements. In fact, the initial year of teaching via your internship or student teaching is replete with tensions. The tensions come with the combination of you—your personality, your prior classroom experiences, your concept of yourself as a teacher—mixed with your teaching context—school placement, cooperating teacher, and university affiliation. These tensions often create anxiety, which distracts student teachers from their primary tasks of learning to teach and becoming a teacher. Such tensions also can lead to preoccupation and in some cases sleeplessness. Although this type of tension may not be resolvable during your first year of teaching, recognizing the tension and acknowledging it as a source of anxiety will prevent you from spending too much emotional energy thinking about it, coping with it, or trying to resolve it. By identifying tensions common to practice teaching and giving examples of how these tensions manifest themselves, I hope to relieve some of your anxiety, thus proving the axiom, "awareness is half the battle."

Deborah Britzman (2003), in her book *Practice Makes Practice,* identifies tensions "between knowing and being, thought and action, theory and practice, knowledge and experience, the technical and the existential, the objective and the subjective" (26). Britzman writes,

> the delicate position in the classroom allows insight into the struggle of voice in both teaching and learning. Marginally situated in two worlds, the student teacher as part student and part teacher has the dual struggle of educating others while being educated. Consequently, student teachers appropriate different voices in the attempt to speak for themselves yet all the while act in a largely inherited and constraining context. This struggle characterizes the tensions between being and becoming a teacher as student teachers draw from their past and present in the process of coming to know. (36)

Britzman describes many contradictions of teaching and learning. I am going to focus on two that confront every student teacher, intern, and teacher candidate.

The First Tension: Becoming the Teacher I Want to Be vs. Fitting In

One of the largest tensions of student teaching is the conflicting realities of becoming the teacher you imagine you want to become and "fitting in," not only with the culture of the school but also the expectations of your cooperating teacher. All of us carry images of the teacher we want to be (and some images of the teacher we do not want to be). This internal image and the desire to become that teacher often come directly into conflict with becoming the teacher that others—faculty and administration at your school placement—expect you to be. When the two conflicting conceptions of "teacher" simultaneously confront the new teachers, they experience anxiety, discomfort, or pain. The new teacher must choose whether to acquiesce, rebel, negotiate, compromise, and so forth.

Here are some comments from teacher candidates in the midst of this tension during the early weeks of their school placements for practice teaching:

- My supervising teacher gives worksheets all the time. I don't want to teach with worksheets.
- I want to wear jeans and a t-shirt, but my university supervisor told me I have to wear a shirt and tie.
- I want the kids to call me Jim, but the principal told me I have to go by Mr. Smith. I made my students read and answer questions from the book today. I thought I'd never do that, and here it is only the second week of my block teaching and I'm giving blah assignments.

As the year progresses, the same tension often appear around instruction and classroom management. Teacher candidates comment:

- My cooperating teacher told me to lead discussions rather than do hands-on activities. She said students learn just as much from discussion, but I think she doesn't like the noise and the desks moved around.
- I had the students in learning groups; they were talking and learning. The principal walked in and I could tell she did not like the conversation.

One of the conflicts common to student teachers is how much noise the student teacher is willing to tolerate versus that level the cooperating teacher will tolerate. The noise question is both an instructional and classroom management issue. It has a lot to do with older and newer philosophies of teaching. In the previous century (especially 1950–1999) learning was thought of as an individual endeavor. Now, we recognize the benefits of people learning together and sharing experiences. In the previous era, learning could be accomplished in quiet; however, group learning requires communication. Tensions arise among older and newer views of education.

Let me share with you one experience I had that resulted in major tension. I wanted to teach a hands-on lesson to engage tactile-kinesthetic students in my classroom. I brought in the manipulatives and taught the lesson. During the lesson it became obvious that the students were not accustomed to breaking into small groups, staying on task, and cleaning up. They were excited and noisy, although they did attend to the engaging activity. Because there was no tradition of hands-on activities in the social studies department, I would have to teach the students how to behave during such activities. I was willing to teach that behavior over a period of weeks; however, my mentor teacher expected the students to be quiet and sit in their seats in rows. She was not willing for me to take the time to teach the students the appropriate behaviors and skills necessary for meaningful learning to take place in hands-on activities in groups. She told me to lead discussions rather than do hands-on activities.

The tension between the two of us mounted. I wanted to do hands-on activities because it addressed equity in my classroom; it engaged the tactile-kinesthetic learners, who rarely got to use their strengths in the classroom. My mentor highly valued an orderly classroom and assigned a lot of seatwork that involved individual listening, reading, and writing. My sense of fairness for the students was violated. In addition, I felt cheated that I would not get the opportunity to develop my skills teaching hands-on lessons. To partially resolve my problem, I worked with two other teachers to develop my skills. Although I had an additional class to prepare, it was worth it. Both teachers let me try new teaching techniques and were there to observe and support me while I tried. They gave me valuable feedback after the lessons.

As supervising professor from a local university, I worked with many student teachers and interns. When it was evident that tensions between mentor teacher and student teacher were not going to clear up, I recommended that the students repeatedly say to themselves. "Next year when I have my own classroom. . . ."

The Second Tension: Theory vs. Praxis

Teacher-preparation programs all exhibit a tension between the students' immediate desire to improve praxis and the faculty's desire that pre-service teachers learn theory and explore the research literature to support professional growth over an entire career. Furthermore, the mentor teacher of the school placement usually favors emphasizing praxis. Although many university professors agree that praxis is important, they also see value in knowing and understanding theory and see themselves as your major source of theory in a praxis-dominant world. Praxis meets scholarship. The two should inform one another. Scholarship should form the basis for praxis; praxis should validate the research or point the way for new scholarship. Nevertheless, the school year moves forward at a relentless pace, and interns feel an urgency to know what and how to teach—tomorrow, "Thursday," or next week.

Although I am an academic who thinks theory is essential to the development and growth of educators, I also know, as a former classroom teacher, that praxis is the teacher's life and demands attention daily. I hope this book will help you jumpstart your own teaching skills and build your confidence so that when you enter the university classroom you can focus on learning theory, strategies of instruction, philosophies of education, and research-based praxis. Educational theory forms a framework on which you can hang your classroom observations. Theory helps you make sense of the multitude of interactions that you see around you, whether those interactions are social or instructional. You observe thousands of interactions daily—students with students, students with teachers, students with administrators, students with learning, and teachers with learning. Theory gives you, the new professional, a framework on which to hang these myriad observations. Theory is analogous to the trunk and branches of a Christmas tree. Your observations become the ornaments and other decorations. Without the branches on which to hang the decorations, you would have a pile of glitz. During his first year of teaching, a colleague of mine, referring to the Christmas tree analogy, said, "That tree is pretty gaudy right now." With time and greater understanding his tree became less gaudy and seemingly more organized. Without theory, you have a jumble of observations that would take years to sort through and make sense of.

Pre-service teachers and faculty who can bridge theory and praxis—acknowledging the value of both—have an easier time interacting and negotiating this particular tension.

Summary

Classroom placements carry with them tensions. These tensions often cause anxiety and may not be resolvable. Two such tensions are:

- Becoming the teacher I want to be vs. fitting in.
- Theory vs. praxis.

Recognizing the tensions and acknowledging them as a source of anxiety will prevent you from spending too much emotional energy thinking about, coping with, or trying to resolve these inherent tensions.

REFERENCES

Britzman, D. P. 2003. *Practice Makes Practice: A critical study of learning to teach.* Revised edition. Albany: State University of New York Press.

Kohl, H. 1985. *Growing Minds: On becoming a teacher.* New York: Harper and Row.

ONLINE RESOURCE

Alsop. J. Teacher identity discourses: Negotiating personal and professional spaces. http://books.google.com/books?id=7bsBOTgTY34C&pg=PA60&lpg=PA60& dq=Tensions+of+student+teaching&source=web&ots=gn4MwGYBIY&sig=x O-9T7KoJ03-zTPD8h9uPf_P6M4&hl=en&sa=X&oi=book_result&resnum= 3&ct=result#PPR7,M1 (accessed January 11, 2009).

Chapter 17

Organizing Your Room to Suit Your Needs

No two classrooms in a school are identical. Although the physical layout of the walls and windows may be the same, each classroom is unique, reflecting the personality of the teacher. Teachers move the desks around, decorate the walls, set procedures, enforce policies, and establish routines that reflect their unique teaching perspectives and personalities. In this chapter, I share my own experience with creating a classroom in which both students and teacher could thrive.

Establishing your classroom policies, routines, and procedures has double benefits. First, it will make your classroom a predictable place for students to learn and work. Second, it will save you energy, patience, and aggravation. For example, if students know they are to always turn in their assignment to the inbox on your desk, there will be less confusion, less student uncertainty, and fewer lost papers. You and your students will spend less time looking for missing assignments and neither of you will have that awful feeling in the pit of your stomach about a missing grade and what to do about it. Setting policy, procedures, and routines early in the school year helps students and teachers get off to a good start.

Preserving Sanity, Good Humor, and Patience

A few things about being a teacher and interacting with students set my nerves on edge. I try to limit or eliminate those situations. For example, one thing I cannot tolerate is a group of students hanging around my desk asking for things important to them but trivial to me. A student's request for adhesive tape while I was signing and recording an absentee form, which could have administrative and grade consequences, was an aggravation. I sought to eliminate the aggravation without being negative to the students. I did three things to make the students more self-sufficient. First, I created a students' table by the door of my classroom. Second, I created a student supply box and placed it on the table.

Third, I created a folder with absent student assignments and also placed it on the table.

The student table was a good idea that met both student and teacher needs. The teacher's desk was my territory, and the students' table was theirs. I placed the students' table by the door to the hallway. It contained hall passes to the office, nurse, library, and guidance office, and a sign-out sheet for leaving the classroom, as well as the student supply box. It also held jackets, textbooks, notebooks, and so forth, which students had left behind; it was a mini lost and found. Students were welcome to hang out and rearrange the contents of the student table, which they were not welcome to do at my desk.

For the student supply box, I found a red plastic box with a lid and filled it with items that students frequently requested—bandages for small cuts, white-out liquid, transparent tape, scissors, markers, colored pencils, a paper punch, and rulers. The students were free to open the box and look for whatever they needed. They also let me know when items needed replenishing.

I also created an absent student work file in which I put worksheets and other assignments for students who were absent. I took a bright yellow folder, labeled it "Absent Student Work," and put it on the student table. If a student was absent, I put the individual's name on a worksheet and put it in the file. I also had a form that I filled out in the event that the assignment did not require a worksheet. The form pictured a person lying on a couch and said, "While you were sick. . . ." I wrote the page number or whatever and stuck it in the file. Students checked the folder when they returned to class. The system reduced the number of students at my desk, freed me from looking in my planner to see what assignment was given when, and reduced the need for looking for the missed worksheets and handouts. The folder saved me a great deal of irritation and work.

These three—students' table, student supply box, and absent student work—prevented students from congregating at my desk and clambering for my attention. This helped preserve my good humor and patience. I encourage you to set up your room to limit the types of things that fray your patience and detract from your ability to teach. Sometimes the solutions are simple.

Managing Papers

To keep students on task, I gave them an assignment each day. When I taught on block schedule with three classes per day, that technique worked well. I had about seventy-five papers to mark and record each day. However, when I taught five classes per day on a traditional schedule, I was overwhelmed with paper.

To tame the paper monster, I bought two stair-step organizers with a slot for each class period. Students turned in their papers to the organizer on the teacher's desk in the slot that corresponded to the period of the day. For all 180 days of the school year, it was the same. No one was confused or uncertain where to turn in their papers, and few papers were lost. After I graded the assignments and entered the scores into the computer, I put the papers into the appropriate slot in the organizer on the students' table. From there students or I could return the papers.

If you are concerned about privacy of grades, especially with students returning papers to others in the class, put the grade on the back of the paper. That way the grade is not immediately evident to the person returning the papers.

All of the organization in the world does not address a fundamental problem of student teachers and interns: how can I do all of this grading and plan for next week at the same time?

Grading Papers

As I mentioned previously, I gave students an assignment every day to keep them on task. The upside was that they did their work and learning progressed; the downside was that I had many papers to grade and grades to record.

During my internship, one experienced teacher passed on a piece of advice that another more experienced teacher taught him. "Just because you collect the papers it does not mean that you have to grade them." That was a revelation to me, and it made perfect sense. Part of teaching is giving students the opportunity to interact with new information and concepts to help transfer them from short-term memory to long-term memory. Just because I gave students an opportunity to interact with information did not mean that I needed to grade the papers and record the resulting scores.

I also gave completion grades for routine assignments that reinforced learning and took only a few minutes to complete—five points if you completed an assignment and zero if you did not. For example, foreign language workbooks often re-teach one skill or one concept (for example, making a noun plural). At the beginning of class, I asked everyone to open their workbooks and show them to me as I passed by their desks. I marked complete or incomplete in the grade book. Then, I showed an overhead transparency of the correct answers, so the students could check their work.

I also requested that students correct their own worksheets and grade them. Correcting their work gave the students one more opportunity to interact with the material. (As you may recall, people need to interact with information about seven times to learn it.) To limit the cheating, I made two rules: first was that I drew papers at random and graded them. If I found a student score was greater than my score, I doubled the number of points wrong. Also, I gave students the opportunity to resubmit homework papers. If they got a poor score, they could resubmit their assignment. My rationale was that if they learned something on their own timelines rather than the teacher's, the learning was still valid. Giving them an opportunity to redo their homework assignments reduced the incentive to cheat. Having students grade their own papers allowed me to spend less time grading and more time planning.

A word of caution about grading. It is important that teachers know what their students know, what they do not know, and their common mistakes. Formative assessment allows you to know these three things on a daily basis. If you allow your students to grade their own papers and you only record the scores, you will not know these things. One reason I allowed the students to grade their own homework was because while they were doing seatwork, I spent the entire time looking over their shoulders, reading papers, and answering questions. I looked at every student's paper. I knew who in my class understood the concepts and could apply them and who could not. I also knew what the most common errors of the day were. When the students corrected their papers from the overhead transparencies, I could point out common errors that I had observed so the students could check their own work more closely. If you decide to use one of the work-saving grading techniques I describe, make sure you are still assessing your students' learning.

Students Leaving the Classroom

In today's society, with frequent discipline problems in schools and a growing concern for student safety, students are not allowed to roam the hallways of schools during class sessions. Students in the hall need passes to whatever their destination. To allow me to concentrate on teaching rather than classroom procedures, I created a pass and sign-out system. With a word processor and clip art, I made hall passes for common destinations: restroom, guidance office, library, and nurse's office. The passes sat on the students' table near the door next to the sign-out sheet. The sign-out sheet asked for name, destination, time in, and time out. Each time a student left the room, s/he had to sign out and carry a pass. Upon return, s/he marked the time on the sign-out sheet. In the event the principal, coach, or counselor needed to know the whereabouts of a student, my records showed it.

Students often get called to the office to talk to guidance counselors and administrators as well as pick up items (for example, textbooks, homework, musical instruments, or lunches) that their parents drop off for them. So that a student's presence in the hallway is immediately recognized as legitimate, students usually carry hall passes. My hall pass with my name on it was 8.5" x 5.5" (a half sheet); the large size made it easily visible in the students' hands as they walked to the office. I laminated the passes with clear contact paper, so they would withstand many uses.

Students requesting permission to leave the classroom to go to the restroom are annoying to a teacher for several reasons. First, such requests break the flow of the lesson. Second, teachers are supposed to read students' minds to determine if the student really needs to go or if they will use the time out of the classroom for another—perhaps a mischievous, dangerous, or harmful—purpose. By the time students get to high school, I figure they can manage their time between classes to use the restroom, but I also know that emergencies do happen, especially to female students. To get around the restroom problem, I simply give each student, at the beginning of the marking period, three restroom passes (see figure 17.1). I instruct the students to depart and arrive quietly. After using their passes, they put them in a designated box on my desk. By the way, students know that restroom trips during tests are not allowed because answers can be found in textbooks in lockers. Restroom passes work great. Students leave and enter the classroom as needed, with few interruptions of the lessons.

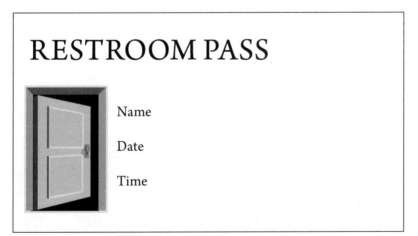

RESTROOM PASS

Name

Date

Time

FIG. 17.1. Restroom Pass.

Late Assignments

When I started teaching, students' excuses for not having homework completed were numerous; many were new to me. The first time a student told me, "I don't have my homework done, we had to take Granny to the emergency room last night," I was astounded by the cultural differences. Where I came from, children and adolescents did not accompany family members to the emergency room. I did not want to have to judge the veracity of this excuse or any other to allow or disallow the late assignment. To avoid the problem, I gave every student in my classes two late-homework passes per term, which they simply stapled to their assignment when they submitted it to my inbox (see figure 17.2). As soon as they received their passes, they signed their names on them. I changed the color of the paper the passes were printed on from one marking period to the next to prevent students from sharing or hoarding their passes and using them in ways I did not intend. Each student decided when to use her/his passes. Some students decided that staying up late to cheer on the school basketball team on Tuesday night was a good reason. Others used theirs when family emergencies hit. The vast majority of students never used their late passes, but somehow just having the option to use one made the students more comfortable in my classroom. The benefit of late homework passes to both the student and the teacher were priceless.

LATE HOMEWORK PASS

Name:

Staple me to your assignment.

FIG. 17.2. Late Homework Pass.

Summary

In this chapter, I share my own experience of creating a classroom so that both students and I could thrive. I describe my efforts to give students their own space—a students' table, a student supply box, and a folder for absentee make-up work. Likewise, I share tips and techniques for organizing and grading student papers to reduce the time spent grading, as well as a system for managing students coming and going from the classroom. I suggest that you think about things that will help you thrive and those things that irritate and annoy you. Then, set up your room to maximize the first and minimize the second. Often, the solutions are simple.

Chapter 18

Developing Your Own Teaching Style

During an introductory teaching methods class, I was encouraging my students to show enthusiasm for the subjects they teach. I cited research showing that students, teachers, and administrators valued enthusiasm and interpersonal relationships more highly than knowledge and organization of subject matter or plans and classroom procedures. After class, a soft-spoken student came to see me. She talked about a high-school teacher who impressed her students by talking about mathematics with such emotion that the teacher had tears in her eyes. We continued chatting about teaching; all the while something seemed to be troubling her. Suddenly, she blurted out, "I could never be an enthusiastic teacher like you." Taken aback, I replied, "I hope not." I continued, "You will develop your own unique teaching style." She seemed relieved. During the ensuing weeks, I witnessed her and her peers develop their self-confidence and their own teaching styles.

The thought of clones of myself teaching in local schools is a horrifying thought. I have a fair number of idiosyncrasies, which I do not want my students to emulate. Although imitation may be the highest form of flattery, teachers need to develop their own styles. Copying another person's style is not fair to you. You need to develop the artistic teacher within yourself.

Teaching styles are as varied as people's personalities. One teacher may arrive in costume and teach with great dynamism. He speaks dramatically, walks around the room, and interacts with his students, eliciting answers even from reticent students. This teacher is spontaneous, changing his lesson to follow the teachable moment. He exhausts himself with the effort. At the other end of the spectrum is the teacher who conserves her energy and movement. She may not step from behind the podium. Her gestures are few and small, and the lesson is carefully structured. She does not deviate from the lesson. Additionally, she uses vivid description, interesting analogies, and examples from around the world to help her students understand. Though quite different, both teachers are effective. Both teachers have a love of their disciplines, effective communication skills, and great people skills.

As you develop your teaching style, remember that many teaching styles are effective. Give yourself the latitude to develop your own. Some mentors have a narrow vision of the variety of styles that will be effective. I have noticed that loud, strict disciplinarians tend to think the best way to control a class is by being loud and strict. Observing other successful teachers shows this to be false. When you observe, experiment, and reflect, you will develop your own effective style. Along the way, you may have a failed lesson or several. A flop, or even a major flop, is normal. You have to take chances and push your skills to get better. Student teachers, interns, and teacher candidates have all expressed that some days are diamonds and some days are dust. If you find yourself in the dust, get up, brush off the dirt, and try again. Tomorrow is a new day.

Though I can predict a teaching style that will be effective in the classroom, I cannot predict which style will not be effective. My first comeuppance in prediction came at the hands of a quiet, middle-aged male student. I thought he could not be outspoken enough to teach energetic and sometimes unruly high school students. He was caring, warm, and fascinated by children, so I suggested he also earn an elementary certificate. Later, he began to student teach at a local high school, and I supervised his progress. He had good interpersonal skills and encouraged his students, yet lacked forceful classroom discipline. The students liked him, however, and started reminding one another to be quiet and pay attention. One day when they were noisy, he wrote "S-H-H-H" on the board in big letters. The students quieted.

This talented man had developed his own teaching style. He inspired the students to help with discipline—his weak area—through the use of excellent interpersonal skills—his strength. I know of no one else who can write S-H-H-H on the board and effectively quiet a class. I salute him for developing his own teaching style.

What is your teaching style? When do you feel best in the classroom? To answer these questions, forget the "Book of Shoulds." The teacher's "Book of Shoulds" is an unwritten code of behavior governing things that teachers traditionally do or are thought to do. For example, teachers give solid lectures; teachers are stern—they may smile but not laugh in class; teachers are the center of attention in a classroom; teachers always know the answers. If I had to develop my teaching style around these traditional misperceptions, I would be miserable, in two ways: I would be a miserable (lousy) teacher and I would feel miserable.

Developing your own style will take time. Follow your intuition and experiment with different techniques; take continuing-education classes to learn other peoples' techniques. With effort, you will create a style that builds on your strengths as a teacher and obscures your weaknesses. You will be able to tell, through your own enjoyment and the positive reaction of your students, that you have found your own style.

Happy teaching!

Afterword

Now that you have read this book, I hope you can go more confidently into your classroom to teach. As you recall, this book was designed to address praxis. Your classroom experience alone probably will not make you a great teacher. Scholarship is an equally important complement of excellent teacher-preparation programs. The two—praxis and scholarship—will help you grow as a professional over your entire career. I challenge you to go to your department, school, faculty, or college of education and fully participate in your classes, grappling with the tough issues associated with providing a quality education for all learners. By "fully participating," I mean engaging totally, not hanging back thinking education courses are less important than your disciplinary courses that you took in your bachelor degree program. Remember, your return often reflects your investment. Ultimately, you want your students to participate and engage fully in your courses, so model that behavior yourself.

Index

Into the Classroom was designed and typeset on a Macintosh computer system 10.6 using InDesign CS5 software. The body text is set in 11.5/13.5 Arno Pro and display type is set in Helvetica Neue. This book was designed and typeset by Barbara Karwhite and manufactured by Thomson-Shore, Inc.